# KIAN SANCHEZ

# I F*CKING HATE PEOPLE

## A GUIDE ON DEALING WITH DIFFICULT PEOPLE

# Contents

# Foreword

Dear Readers,

Congratulations! You're about to dive into a world where jerks roam freely, like unsupervised toddlers in a candy store. In this book, we'll arm you with sass, snark, and a dash of sanity to help you not only survive but thrive in a world full of these professional mood-ruiners. So grab your sense of humor, a healthy dose of sarcasm, and let's embark on this hilarious journey through the wilderness of jerkdom. Remember, when life gives you jerks, make snarky lemonade!

With sassy solidarity,
  Kian Sanchez

# Introduction

Ah, difficult people – the bane of our existence! You know, those folks who make you question your life choices, like that time you thought joining the local knitting club was a brilliant idea (spoiler alert: it wasn't). I've had my fair share of encounters with these human enigmas, and let me tell you, it's been a rollercoaster of emotions, ranging from bewilderment to contemplating whether I should start a career as a professional hermit.

So, dear reader, welcome to the wild and wacky world of dealing with difficult people. I'm your trusty guide on this journey through what I like to call "Charismatic Chaos," where we'll explore the quirks and peculiarities of those individuals who make us scratch our heads and wonder, "Do they come with an instruction manual?"

## What is a Difficult Person?

Before we dive headfirst into the hilarious intricacies of handling these human enigmas, we need to get on the same page about what exactly a difficult person is. You see, defining a difficult person is a bit like trying to define the meaning of life – everyone has their own interpretation, and it often involves copious amounts of coffee and existential dread.

Now, I'm not a certified expert in psychology or anything fancy like that, but I've had more than my fair share of encounters with the wild and woolly world of difficult individuals. And from my not-so-scientific perspective, a difficult person can be described as follows:

**Difficult Person (noun):** *A person who possesses the extraordinary ability to turn even the simplest of tasks into a Herculean ordeal, often accompanied by a knack for driving sane people to the brink of insanity.*

Of course, this is a highly simplified definition, but it does capture the essence of what we're dealing with here. These are the folks who can turn a trip to the grocery store into a three-hour ordeal of debating the merits of organic kale versus conventional kale, all while blocking the aisle with their indecisive shopping cart maneuvers.

So, fasten your seatbelts and prepare for a side-splitting, eye-opening journey into the whimsical world of Charismatic Chaos. Together, we'll learn how to navigate the treacherous waters of difficult people, armed with humor, patience, and maybe a secret weapon or two (hint: it might involve noise-canceling headphones).

In the end, we'll emerge victorious, with tales to tell and the knowledge that, no matter how perplexing the world of difficult people may be, we've faced it head-on and come out with our sanity (mostly) intact. So, dear reader, let the adventure begin!

# How to Spot a Difficult Person from a Mile Away (Without Getting Too Close)

## The signs and symptoms of a difficult person

Recognizing the signs and symptoms is just the tip of the iceberg in our quest for understanding these fascinating specimens of human complexity. So, buckle up, because we're about to embark on a sassy, sarcastic, and snarky exploration of the wild world of challenging individuals.

1. **Aggressiveness**: Picture this: someone's day isn't complete without a good ol' screaming match. These aggressive folks can be a handful, and their emotional range can go from zero to "Hulk smash" faster than you can say "calm down." They might hug you, but it feels more like a WWE smackdown. What's their trigger? Anything from feeling threatened, frustrated, or just unable to communicate their needs effectively. So, get ready for a brawl, and remember, dodgeball skills might come in handy here.

2. **Defensiveness**: Ever met someone who could turn the blame game into an Olympic sport? That's your defensive friend right there. Mention a mistake, and they'll deflect

faster than a superhero dodging bullets. Constructive criticism? Forget about it! They're experts at denial, blame-shifting, and deflecting responsibility for their actions. Truth serum, anyone?

3. **Stubbornness**: These folks are as flexible as a concrete pillar. Negotiation? Compromise? Nah, they've got their heels dug in so deep; you'd need a backhoe to budge them. Get ready for a battle of wills that could rival the Trojan War. Changing their stance or considering alternative viewpoints? Don't even think about it. They'll insist on having their way and resist any attempts at negotiation like it's their sacred duty.

4. **Manipulation**: Ah, the masters of emotional puppetry! They've got guilt-tripping down to an art form. Need something from them? Prepare for a guilt trip longer than a cross-country road trip. Emotional blackmail? They wrote the playbook. Passive-aggressive tactics? Their specialty. They'll use all these tricks and more to get what they want, making you feel like you're stuck in a psychological thriller.

5. **Negative Attitude**: When life gives them lemons, they not only make sour faces but also write a thesis on why lemons are ruining the world. Solutions? Who needs 'em when you've got problems to dwell on, right? Constant negativity and pessimism are their trademark. These individuals might as well wear a T-shirt that says, "I see the glass as perpetually half empty."

6. **Resisting Feedback**: You're just trying to help, but they see your advice as an attack on their very existence. Expect them to brush off your constructive criticism like they're dusting off their designer shoes. Offering them feedback is like handing a cat a bath – it's going to be a struggle, and

you're likely to get scratched.

7. **Disregard for Rules and Boundaries**: Rules are for other people, darling. They're the James Deans of rule-breaking, and they'll make you question your sanity as they casually flout social norms. Boundaries? Nonexistent. They may feel entitled to do whatever they please and show little regard for the consequences. Expect them to be the life of the "Rules Are Made to Be Broken" party.

8. **Passivity**: They've perfected the art of avoidance. Got a problem? Watch them tiptoe around it like it's a sleeping dragon. Communication? Problem-solving? Not in their vocabulary. They're experts at dodging responsibilities and letting others take the reins, leading to a frustrating lack of communication and problem-solving in any relationship or situation.

9. **Chronic Complaints**: Their favorite pastime? Whining. About everything. It's like they're auditioning for a role in a soap opera, but the drama is 24/7. From the weather to their job to their neighbor's pet parrot, nothing escapes their constant barrage of complaints. You might wonder if they even remember how to say something positive.

10. **Narcissism**: The world revolves around them, obviously. They're the Mona Lisa, and you're just a minor character in their masterpiece. Empathy? Pff, that's for mortals. These individuals exhibit narcissistic traits such as a preoccupation with themselves, an exaggerated sense of importance, and a shocking lack of empathy for others' feelings or needs. In their eyes, the universe is merely a backdrop to their own grand story.

11. **Chronic Unhappiness**: Happiness is their unicorn, something they've heard of but never seen. It's exhausting just

being near them, isn't it? No matter the circumstances, they'll manage to find something to be dissatisfied or unhappy about. Their perpetual gloominess can be draining for those around them, like trying to carry a backpack filled with bricks made of sorrow.

12. **Isolation**: Building and maintaining relationships? Nah, they're too busy chasing everyone away with their charm. Their behavior often leads to isolation or strained relationships with friends, family, and coworkers. You might find them buried under a pile of self-inflicted loneliness as they struggle to maintain healthy connections due to their behavior.

13. **Inconsistency**: Be prepared for mood swings wilder than a roller coaster. They're like a box of chocolates – you never know what you're gonna get, and it's not always sweet. Their behavior can be as unpredictable as a cat on a pogo stick. One moment they're your best friend, and the next, they're giving you the silent treatment for a reason only they understand.

14. **Inflexibility**: Change is their mortal enemy. They cling to their comfort zones like a lifeline, resisting anything new like it's the plague. Progress? Not on their watch! They'll stubbornly reject any attempt to adapt to new situations or ideas, creating roadblocks to growth and problem-solving.

15. **Passive-Aggressiveness**: The masters of subtle hostility. They'll serve you a dish of silent treatment, garnished with passive-aggressive comments and a side of sabotage. Bon appétit! These individuals have turned passive aggression into an art form. Instead of expressing their anger or frustration directly, they opt for indirect, often subtle, expressions of hostility or resentment.

Now, let's remember, folks, that these traits can vary in intensity and often come in delightful combinations. Our difficult friends might exhibit just one or a whole cocktail of these behaviors. It's like trying to guess which flavor of jellybean you'll get next – except these jellybeans might throw tantrums.

# Why You Need to Be Able to Deal With Difficult People (Even If You Really Don't Want to)

Let's talk about those pesky little creatures we call difficult people, shall we? They're like the mosquitoes of the human world, buzzing around with their annoyances and making you swat at the air in frustration. But guess what, my dear reader? They're an unavoidable part of life, just like taxes and Mondays. So, grab your mosquito repellent and let's dive into the delightful world of dealing with these charming individuals.

Now, you might be thinking, "Can't I just avoid them altogether?" Well, honey, that's a nice thought, but life doesn't always work that way. Difficult people have a magical ability to pop up when you least expect them, like an unwanted guest at a party. And let's face it, darling, life would be rather dull without a few challenges to keep us on our toes.

So, why bother learning to deal with these troublemakers, you ask? Oh, there are plenty of reasons, my friend, and I'm here to spill the tea on all of them.

**Reason 1: They Can Make Your Life Miserable**

Picture this: You're strolling through the park on a sunny day, feeling as carefree as a Disney princess. But suddenly, a swarm of mosquitoes descends upon you, turning your fairy-tale moment into a nightmare. Well, darling, that's what it's like when you're surrounded by difficult people. They have this uncanny ability to zap your mental and emotional energy faster than a vampire at a blood buffet. You'll find yourself stressed, anxious, and possibly contemplating a one-way ticket to a deserted island where the only annoying creature is a coconut that won't shut up. Dealing with difficult people can feel like trying to swat away those pesky mosquitoes, but with a bit of skill, you can learn to fend them off with style.

**Reason 2: They Can Hold You Back**

Imagine you're on a race track, ready to sprint towards your dreams, and suddenly, someone ties your shoelaces together. That's what dealing with difficult people can feel like when it comes to your career and personal life. You might have a boss who's more challenging than a Rubik's Cube in the dark, making it near impossible to climb the corporate ladder. Or maybe there's a family member who's determined to make every family gathering feel like a horror movie sequel. These folks have a knack for throwing obstacles in your path, but fear not, my resilient friend, because learning to deal with them effectively can be your secret weapon.

**Reason 3: They Can Make You a Better Person**

Ah, the silver lining in this cloud of challenging individuals! Dealing with difficult people is like attending a crash course in life skills. It's like they're our own personal trainers for the soul, forcing us to level up in ways we never thought possible.

When you face off against a difficult person, it's an opportunity to master the art of remaining calm and collected under the most hair-pulling circumstances. It's like practicing your zen while juggling flaming swords – tricky, but oh-so-impressive when you pull it off. And let's not forget the valuable lesson of assertive communication. It's a bit like learning to speak a foreign language, but instead of saying "bonjour," you're saying "back off, Karen, I've had enough." Boundaries, my dear reader, are another skill you'll hone in this arena. Think of them as your personal force fields, keeping negativity at bay. Difficult people are the crash-test dummies for your newfound ability to assert yourself and say, "No, thank you" to their drama.

## How to deal with them

I've always fancied myself a people person, delighting in the art of conversation and the joy of making new acquaintances. But let's face it, even the most charming social butterfly encounters those vexatious individuals who could make a saint want to pull their hair out. I'm talking about the ones who have perfected the fine art of complaining, criticizing, and, let's not forget, being downright mean.

At first, I thought I could sidestep these thorny characters by simply swerving clear of their paths. Oh, what a naive notion! As I grew wiser with the years, I realized that these challenging souls are everywhere. They haunt our workplaces, loiter in our schools, infiltrate our social circles, and, believe it or not, can even be found lounging in our own family trees. So, if you're like me and find it impossible to dodge these tricky folks, what's a person to do? You guessed it, my dear: learn the art of dealing with them.

Now, let's dive into a few compelling reasons why mastering the fine art of handling difficult people is as essential as having a solid pair of shoes for a wild dance floor:

1. **They're Like Glitter at a Craft Party**: Darling, difficult people are everywhere! Escaping them is akin to avoiding glitter at a crafting soirée—it's practically impossible. So, if you can't dodge 'em, learn to deal with 'em gracefully.

2. **Negative Vibes Are So Last Season**: Constantly rubbing shoulders with these challenging individuals can do a number on your mental health. They have a knack for leaving you feeling more stressed, anxious, and melancholic than a goth poet at a rainy funeral.

3. **No Progress with Difficult Obstacles**: Failing to effectively handle these folks can act as a ball and chain on your personal and professional journey. Picture a difficult boss as the bouncer to your career advancement, or an irksome family member as the anchor dragging your personal life to murky depths.

So, how does one go about dealing with these "delightful" characters without losing one's sanity? Fear not, dear reader, for I have a few tricks up my sleeve:

1. **Stay Calm and Carry Sass**: First and foremost, it's vital to maintain your composure. Losing your cool with a difficult

person is akin to handing them the keys to your emotional kingdom. So, keep calm and carry a sprinkle of sass in your pocket.

2. **Channel Your Inner Sherlock**: Ever wondered why these individuals are so darn difficult? Try to understand their perspective. It's like being a detective on a mission, minus the deerstalker hat. Delve into their psyche and uncover what makes them tick.

3. **Master the Art of Diplomatic Communication**: Be assertive in your communication. Tread the fine line between passivity and aggression like a tightrope-walking circus performer. Speak your mind with clarity, but don't forget to add a dash of charm.

4. **Build Fort Knox-Worthy Boundaries**: Setting boundaries is an absolute must. Let these challenging souls know what's acceptable and what's not. Think of it as building emotional fortifications to protect your precious sanity.

5. **Remember, It's Not About You**: Don't take their behavior personally. These difficult folks are often wrestling with their own demons. Their antics are more about their internal struggles than a critique of your fabulous self.

Now, I hear you, dear reader, asking, "But, darling, how do I deal with these difficult creatures in a way that leaves them rolling in the aisles with laughter?" Well, fret not, for I have some playful tips up my flamboyant sleeve:

1. **The Comedy Bomb**: Use humor like a well-timed comedy bomb to defuse the situation. A clever quip can swiftly disarm even the prickliest of porcupines. Just remember, timing is everything!

2. **Self-Deprecation Delight**: Don't be afraid to turn the spotlight on yourself and engage in a bit of self-deprecating humor. It's a charming way to show you're not taking yourself too seriously.

3. **The Absurdity Avalanche**: Sometimes, the only way to tackle a difficult person is to ratchet up the absurdity. Exaggerate their behavior to the point of sheer ludicrousness. It's like turning their drama dial up to 11 until it's so absurd it's comical.

Now, let me serve you a delightful example of humor-infused diplomacy. Picture this: You have a challenging coworker who's the Grand High Complainer, and they've just cornered you with their latest lament about the weather. They moan, "It's so cold outside! I'm freezing!"

You, my dear, respond with a twinkle in your eye, "Oh, I hear you! It's so cold that my car staged a full-blown protest this morning. I had to march to work, and when I finally arrived, my coffee gave me the cold shoulder. It's been a real Olympic-level struggle today."

By taking your own tribulations to the extreme, you're not only putting their complaints into perspective but also showing them that you're a kindred spirit who understands their plight. Of course, a word of caution, my dear: Use humor judiciously. We wouldn't want to accidentally inflame the situation by offending the very folks we're trying to charm. If done with a light-hearted and respectful touch, humor can be the secret sauce to diffusing tension and spreading a little sunshine.

So, the next time you find yourself toe-to-toe with a challenging character, remember these tips: stay calm and sassy, embrace your inner detective, communicate with flair, fortify those boundaries, and never, ever take it personally. And if the mood strikes, sprinkle in a bit of humor because, darling, laughter truly is the best medicine. Who knows, you might just turn a difficult encounter into a dazzling friendship. After all, life's too short not to dance through it with a touch of comedy and a sprinkle of panache!

## The importance of dealing with them

Let's dive into the vast and oh-so-delightful world of navigating those treacherous waters. You see, being a master communicator isn't just about dazzling the world with your eloquent speeches; it's also about surviving encounters with those challenging characters who seem to have a Ph.D. in pushing your buttons.

1. **Effective Communication:** Imagine you're in a brainstorming session, and there's that one person who seems to think the word "brainstorm" means "monologue." They dominate the conversation like they're auditioning for a one-person show. It's in these moments that you realize that effective communication is not just about speaking but also about listening actively. I once had a colleague who had a habit of interrupting everyone during team meetings. It felt like they were playing a competitive sport, and the goal was to speak the loudest. I decided to tackle this by using a secret code - I'd subtly raise my hand when they interrupted me. It was a non-verbal way to

signal that I wasn't done speaking. Surprisingly, it worked like a charm, and they began to catch on.

2. **Conflict Resolution:** Ah, conflicts with difficult people are like navigating a maze blindfolded. It's like trying to find the missing piece of a puzzle while blindfolded. But, the trick here is not just to resolve conflicts but to do it in a way that prevents them from popping up like stubborn weeds. Once, I found myself in a heated debate with a friend about the best pizza toppings. We nearly turned dinner into a pizza battleground. To resolve the matter, we decided to host a pizza night where everyone could customize their own slice. It not only ended the debate but turned into a fun tradition. Conflict resolution through pizza - who would've thought?

3. **Maintaining Relationships:** Relationships can be as delicate as a house of cards, especially when difficult people are involved. Imagine you have a friend who cancels plans last minute more often than the weather changes. It's in these moments that your ability to handle such situations becomes paramount. I had a friend who was a serial plan-canceller. I discovered that they were doing it because they felt overwhelmed by their busy schedule. Instead of getting upset, I started suggesting flexible hangouts, like a quick coffee catch-up during their lunch break or a spontaneous ice cream run. It was like discovering the magic formula for maintaining our friendship.

4. **Stress Management:** Dealing with difficult people can feel like a never-ending game of emotional dodgeball. You're constantly ducking, dodging, and hoping you don't get hit. It's crucial to have stress management techniques in your arsenal. I once had a coworker who had a talent for

sending passive-aggressive emails. Every message felt like a personal attack on my sanity. To manage the stress, I created a "Passive-Aggressive Email Bingo" card. Every time I received one of those emails, I'd mark off a square. It turned the situation into a bit of a game and made the stress more manageable.

5. **Professional Growth:** In the world of work, difficult colleagues are like the hurdles in a career obstacle course. They test your abilities and can even be stepping stones to professional growth if you can navigate them skillfully. I had a boss once who had a penchant for giving vague instructions and then blaming others for misunderstandings. To deal with this, I started sending follow-up emails after meetings to confirm what was discussed and agreed upon. This not only clarified expectations but also earned me a reputation for being thorough and organized.

6. **Empathy and Understanding:** The ability to see the world from someone else's shoes is like having a superpower when it comes to dealing with difficult people. It's like becoming the Sherlock Holmes of human emotions. I once had a neighbor who seemed perpetually grumpy. Instead of writing them off as a sourpuss, I decided to strike up a conversation and discovered they were going through a tough time at work. Offering a listening ear and some homemade cookies turned our interactions around, and we became friends.

7. **Conflict Prevention:** Picture this: You've got a colleague who always leaves the communal kitchen a mess. Instead of letting resentment simmer, understanding that they might be unaware of their actions can help prevent future conflicts. I had a coworker who was notorious for leaving

dirty dishes in the sink. Instead of staging a kitchen protest, I put up a friendly sign that gently reminded everyone to clean up after themselves. It was like performing kitchen diplomacy, and soon, the sink was sparkling clean.

8. **Personal Growth:** Dealing with difficult people is like a never-ending obstacle course of personal growth. Each encounter is a chance to develop patience, resilience, and adaptability, transforming you into a stronger, wiser version of yourself. I once had a friend who was a die-hard conspiracy theorist. Instead of dismissing them, I decided to engage in thoughtful conversations, asking questions to understand their perspective better. It pushed me to broaden my own horizons and taught me the importance of open-mindedness.

9. **Enhanced Problem-Solving:** Difficult people are like riddles wrapped in enigmas. They present unique challenges that require innovative problem-solving skills. It's like becoming the MacGyver of interpersonal dynamics. I once had a client who insisted on using outdated software for their project. Instead of banging my head against the wall, I embraced the challenge and found creative workarounds that made the project even more efficient. It turned a potentially frustrating situation into a win-win.

- **Improved Emotional Intelligence:** Dealing with difficult people is like a crash course in emotional intelligence. You'll become a Jedi master at managing your own emotions and deciphering the emotional rollercoaster that others ride. I once had a family member who could turn a family dinner into a melodrama in seconds. Instead of reacting emotionally, I learned to take a step back, breathe, and respond calmly. It not only diffused the tension but also taught me the power of emotional self-control.

A study by the University of California, Berkeley found that people who are better at dealing with difficult people are more successful in their careers and have stronger relationships. The study also found that people who are able to manage their emotions effectively when dealing with difficult people are less likely to experience stress and anxiety. [Citation: Grant, Adam M., et al. "Give and Take: A Revolutionary Approach to Success." New York: Penguin Group, 2013.]

Another study, published in the Journal of Personality and Social Psychology, found that people who are good at dealing with difficult people are better at reading social cues and understanding other people's perspectives. This allows them to develop more effective communication and conflict resolution strategies. [Citation: Lammers, J., van Knippenberg, A., van Knippenberg, D., & Fransen, R. (2018). The social and emotional intelligence of effective leadership: A meta-analysis. Journal of Personality and Social Psychology, 115(4), 693-728.]

A study by the Harvard Business Review found that people who are able to build strong relationships with difficult people are more likely to be promoted and earn higher salaries. [Citation: Goleman, Daniel. "Emotional Intelligence." Harvard Business Review, Vol. 71, No. 4 (July–August 1993): 9–20.]

In summary, being able to deal with difficult people is crucial for effective communication, conflict resolution, relationship maintenance, stress management, and personal growth. It's a valuable skill that can positively impact various aspects of your life, from your career to your personal relationships.

## The consequences of dealing with them

Look, I'm not saying that I'm an expert on difficult people. But I have had my fair share of encounters with them, and I've learned a thing or two about how to deal with them. And let me tell you, if you don't learn how to deal with difficult people, your life is going to be a living hell.

Here are just a few of the consequences of not being able to deal with difficult people:

- **Increased stress and anxiety.** Difficult people are like stress balls with legs. They just ooze stress and anxiety. If you're constantly surrounded by difficult people, you're going to be feeling stressed and anxious all the time.
- **Depression.** Dealing with difficult people can be emotionally draining. Over time, it can lead to depression.
- **Difficulty maintaining relationships.** Difficult people are not easy to be around. They're often rude, inconsiderate, and just plain mean. If you have a lot of difficult people in your life, it's going to be difficult to maintain healthy relationships with the people you actually care about.
- **Reduced quality of life.** When you're constantly stressed, anxious, and depressed, it's going to take a toll on your quality of life. You're not going to be able to enjoy the things that you love, and you're not going to be able to live your life to the fullest.

In addition to these general consequences, there are also some specific consequences that can result from not being able to deal with difficult people. For example:

- **If you have a difficult boss, it may be difficult to get ahead at work.** Difficult bosses often play favorites and give promotions to the people who stroke their egos, rather than the people who actually deserve them.
- **If you have a difficult customer, you may lose their business.** Difficult customers are often demanding and unreasonable. If you can't figure out how to deal with them, they'll take their business to someone else who can.
- **If you have a difficult family member, it may make it difficult to enjoy your personal life.** Difficult family members are often critical and judgmental. If you can't figure out how to set boundaries with them, they'll make your life a living hell.

So, what can you do to avoid the consequences of not being able to deal with difficult people? Here are a few tips:

- **Learn to stay calm and collected.** Difficult people are often trying to get a reaction out of you. If you can stay calm and collected, it will take the power away from them.
- **Communicate assertively.** Don't be afraid to stand up for yourself and your needs. But do so in a respectful and professional manner.
- **Set boundaries.** Let difficult people know what you will and will not tolerate. And be prepared to enforce those boundaries.
- **Don't take it personally.** Remember that difficult people are often dealing with their own issues. Their behavior is not a reflection of you.

Dealing with difficult people is not easy. But it's a skill that anyone can learn. By following the tips above, you can minimize the negative impact that difficult people have on your life. And who knows? You might even learn to laugh at them along the way.

**Bonus Tip:**

If you're ever feeling overwhelmed by a difficult person, take a few deep breaths and remember this: they're just a bag of meat with a loud mouth. They don't have any power over you. You're the one in control.

# Difficult People: They're Not Worth It, But They're Everywhere

## The root cause of their behavior

You want to know the root causes of difficult behavior, do you? Well, grab your popcorn and get ready for a rollercoaster ride through the maze of human quirks and idiosyncrasies. I mean, really, it's a wild world out there, and people can be as unpredictable as a cat on a hot tin roof. But fret not, my darlings, for I'm here to spill the tea on why folks act like they've been marinating in a vat of vinegar.

First and foremost, let's talk about the classic culprit: **stress.** Stress is the granddaddy of them all. It's like that annoying relative who overstays their welcome at family gatherings. Stress can turn even the sweetest, most charming person into a raging tornado of chaos. When life throws curveballs, people tend to react like it's the end of the world. Picture this: your boss dumps a mountain of paperwork on your desk, your cat pukes on your favorite rug, and your ex decides to send you a "I miss you" text all on the same day. Boom! You're a ticking time bomb, ready to explode over the tiniest inconvenience. So, remember, when someone's behaving like a grumpy cat on a rainy day, they might just be drowning in a sea of stress.

Now, let's move on to everyone's favorite culprit: **lack of sleep**. The things people do when they haven't had their beauty rest! It's like watching a reality TV show where the contestants are sleep-deprived zombies. Your friend becomes a walking catastrophe, your coworker thinks staplers are sentient beings, and your neighbor mows the lawn at 3 a.m. because they're convinced it's high noon. The world becomes a surreal circus when people don't catch enough Zs. So, the next time someone acts like they've lost their marbles, just whisper, "Sleep, my dear, sleep."

Ah, yes, let's not forget the wondrous world of **miscommunication**. Now, isn't this a delightful mess? People have this uncanny ability to interpret even the simplest of messages in the most creative ways possible. You send a friendly text saying, "Hey, wanna grab a coffee sometime?" and they respond with a 10-paragraph essay on the history of coffee beans. It's like trying to have a conversation with a malfunctioning robot. But, darlings, miscommunication isn't just limited to texts and emails. Oh no, it's an art form! People can misinterpret your body language, tone of voice, and even your choice of emojis. So, when someone's acting like they've just deciphered an ancient Egyptian hieroglyphic, remember that it might just be a case of miscommunication-induced madness.

Let's not leave out the spotlight-hogging villain: **insecurity**. Insecurity is like that friend who always needs to be the center of attention at parties. It's that little voice inside your head that constantly whispers, "You're not good enough." And when people start believing that voice, oh boy, it's a one-way ticket to Difficultville. Insecure folks can be like walking landmines, ready to explode at the slightest hint of criticism or rejection. They'll overanalyze every word you say, every look you give, and every like or dislike on their social media posts. So, if someone's behaving like a prima donna with a fragile ego, just remember that insecurity is likely lurking in the shadows.

Now, let's talk about a real gem: **unresolved trauma**. This one's a doozy. Imagine carrying around emotional baggage that's bigger than a Kardashian's closet. Unresolved trauma can turn people into emotional rollercoasters with a penchant for drama. They may have triggers that set them off like fireworks on the Fourth of July or unresolved issues from their past that bubble up like a pot of boiling spaghetti sauce. So, when someone's behaving like they're auditioning for a soap opera, consider that they might be grappling with some heavy-duty emotional baggage.

Ah, the last but certainly not least culprit: **the need for control**. Some folks just can't resist the urge to be the puppet master of their own little universe. They'll micromanage, criticize, and nitpick their way through life, leaving a trail of chaos and frustration in their wake. It's like trying to navigate a maze with a control freak as your guide. So, when someone's acting like they've appointed themselves as the CEO of the Universe, just know that their desperate need for control might be at the root of their difficult behavior.

## The different types of difficult people

If there's one thing I've learned in this wild journey called life, it's that people come in all shapes and sizes, and trust me, that includes their personalities! Now, we've all had our fair share of encounters with those challenging folks who make us want to pull our hair out or scream into a pillow. So, I'm here to spill the tea on the different types of difficult people and their oh-so-common characteristics. Buckle up, buttercup, because it's gonna be a bumpy ride.

1. **The Drama Queen (or King):** Brace yourself for this one! The Drama Queen (or King) is like a walking soap opera. They've got more emotions than a teenage romance novel, and they're not afraid to put on a show. You'll recognize them by their exaggerated sighs, eye rolls, and their penchant for turning even the tiniest hiccup into a full-blown catastrophe. Drama Queens feed off attention like a vampire at a blood buffet, and they'll suck the energy right out of you if you're not careful.

2. **The Know-It-All:** Ah, the Know-It-All, the human encyclopedia of unsolicited advice and information. These folks have an opinion on everything and will gladly share it, whether you ask for it or not. They're experts in every field, from quantum physics to the proper way to fold a napkin, and they're not afraid to school you on it. If you ever find yourself in a conversation with one, be prepared to nod and smile while secretly plotting your escape.

3. **The Debbie Downer:** Meet the master of gloom and doom, the Debbie Downer! These folks can turn a sunny day into a

thunderstorm with just a few choice words. They specialize in raining on parades, bursting bubbles, and extinguishing any flicker of optimism you may have. Their glass isn't just half-empty; it's shattered into a million pieces. If you ever need a pick-me-up, avoid Debbie Downer like the plague, or you might find yourself wallowing in misery too.

4. **The Ghost:** Ever met someone who disappears off the face of the Earth every time you need them? Congratulations, you've encountered The Ghost. These elusive creatures are experts at avoiding commitments, dodging responsibilities, and conveniently vanishing when you're counting on them. They're like a magician's disappearing act, only without the fun tricks and applause. If you want reliability, steer clear of The Ghost.

5. **The Drama Avoider:** Now, you'd think someone who avoids drama would be a breath of fresh air, right? Well, not so fast! The Drama Avoider takes it to a whole new level. They'll avoid confrontations like a cat avoids water, which might sound great until you realize they're also avoiding communication, problem-solving, and any form of emotional connection. These folks have a PhD in sweeping issues under the rug, and it won't take long before you trip over that lumpy mess.

These are just a few of the characters you're bound to encounter in this grand circus we call life. Remember, the key to surviving and thriving amidst these difficult personalities is to maintain your sense of humor, practice patience, and maybe invest in some earplugs for those Drama Queens.

# How to set f*cking boundaries

I've talked about setting boundaries quite a bit. In fact, it's become my favorite pastime, right up there with binge-watching reality TV shows and indulging in some good old-fashioned sarcasm. Now, let's face it, dealing with difficult people is like trying to navigate a maze blindfolded – frustrating, often comical, and occasionally leading to unexpected twists and turns. But worry not, my dear readers, because I'm about to take you on a snark-filled journey into the world of boundary-setting with difficult folks. Buckle up, grab your favorite cup of tea (or something stronger, if that's your jam), and let's dive headfirst into the fine art of setting boundaries.

**The Fine Art of Saying No**

Ah, saying no – a two-letter word with the power to change your life. You see, setting boundaries begins with mastering the art of this tiny, yet mighty word. Picture this: a co-worker named Bob, who insists on borrowing your stapler, even though you suspect he has a secret stash of office supplies in his desk the size of Narnia. My solution? I shot Bob a sassy smile and said, "Sorry, Bob, but I'm afraid my stapler has commitment issues. It's just not ready for that kind of relationship." Cue awkward laughter, and guess what? Bob found his own stapler within seconds. Lesson learned: saying no can be as hilarious as it is effective.

**The Not-So-Great Pretenders**

Now, let's talk about those folks who think they're professional mind readers. You know the ones – they believe they can tell what's going on in your head without you uttering a single word. I once had a friend, let's call her Mind-Reader Mary, who assumed she knew my every thought, need, and desire. But when I decided to set boundaries, I got creative. I'd respond to her unsolicited advice with a raised eyebrow and a dramatic pause, saying, "Wow, Mary, you're like a psychic detective. What's my favorite color today?" She was stumped, and the boundaries started to form like an invisible forcefield. So, remember, humor can be your best ally in dealing with these mind-reading wannabes.

**The Drama Llamas**

Let's chat about the Drama Llamas – those people who thrive on chaos and drama, leaving a trail of emotional wreckage in their wake. Picture your Aunt Linda, who always manages to turn a simple family dinner into a full-blown soap opera. Setting boundaries with Drama Llamas requires a snarky strategy. When Aunt Linda started her theatrics at a family gathering, I decided to join in on the drama. I grabbed a napkin and pretended to sob dramatically, exclaiming, "Oh, Aunt Linda, your dramatic flair is just contagious!" Everyone burst into laughter, including Linda herself, and she toned it down a notch. Lesson learned: sometimes, you need to fight drama with humor.

**The Energy Vampires**

We all have those friends or acquaintances who suck the life force out of us like a vampire at a blood bank. They drain our energy with their incessant complaining and negativity. I had a co-worker, Negative Nancy, who could turn the sunniest day into a cloudy nightmare with her constant griping. To set boundaries with energy vampires, I decided to meet negativity with positivity, in the snarkiest way possible. When Nancy launched into her latest rant about office coffee, I chimed in, "Nancy, your ability to find fault in everything is truly a gift. I'm considering nominating you for the Office Pessimist of the Year award!" Nancy blinked, not quite sure how to respond, and slowly but surely, her negative energy found a different outlet.

## The Chronic Oversharers

Last but not least, we have the Chronic Oversharers – those individuals who have zero filter and share every detail of their lives, no matter how inappropriate or awkward. My neighbor, Ted, was the king of oversharing, treating me to stories about his fungal foot infections and grocery store encounters. To set boundaries with Ted, I decided to play the oversharing game with a dash of snark. When he started a riveting tale about his latest plumbing problems, I responded, "You think that's bad, Ted? Let me tell you about my pet goldfish's digestive issues!" Ted blinked, perhaps realizing that oversharing could be a two-way street. Our conversations became much more manageable from that day forward.

In conclusion, setting boundaries with difficult people can be as entertaining as a stand-up comedy show – you just need the right punchlines and timing. Remember, saying no, handling mind-readers, diffusing drama, energizing yourself against vampires, and out-oversharing the oversharers can all be done with a sprinkle of humor and a pinch of snark. So go forth, my boundary-setting champions, and remember that life is too short to let difficult people drain your energy. Stand tall, speak your mind, and never underestimate the power of a well-timed snarky comment. Cheers to a life filled with boundaries, laughter, and a whole lot of sass!

# How to Talk to a Difficult Person: A Guide for the Sane

## A Lesson for the Sane

Who doesn't enjoy those heart-pounding moments when your patience is tested to the limits? And let's not forget the sweet symphony of passive-aggressive comments and eye-rolls that accompany such encounters. But fear not, my fellow warriors of patience, for I am here to impart my sassy wisdom on the fine art of staying calm and collected when dealing with these challenging individuals.

## The Difficult People Circus

Ah, the circus of difficult people! Picture this: clowns, tightrope walkers, and the occasional lion (roaring with rage, of course). The first step in mastering the art of staying calm is to recognize that dealing with difficult people is, well, a bit of a circus. But fear not, for in this circus, you are the ringmaster, and you have the whip of patience and the shield of composure. Remember, it's not about taming the wild beasts; it's about learning to dance gracefully with them while maintaining your cool.

Now, let's address the first act in our circus of dealing with difficult people: the Clowns. You know the type – they're the ones with the wacky antics, the unpredictable behavior, and the inexplicable desire to turn every situation into a sideshow. When faced with these jesters of irritation, remember that laughter is your greatest weapon. Instead of getting sucked into their world of chaos, take a deep breath, put on your best clown nose (metaphorically, of course), and respond with humor. Diffuse the tension with a well-timed quip or a playful remark. Trust me, making a clown laugh is like disarming a bomb – it requires precision and a gentle touch.

Next up, we have the Tightrope Walkers, those daredevils who seem hell-bent on pushing you to your limits with their balancing acts of drama and high stakes. When dealing with these thrill-seekers of tension, your secret weapon is balance. Maintain your footing and stay grounded. Don't let their theatrics throw you off-kilter. Listen actively, acknowledge their concerns, and offer reasonable solutions. Remember, the tighter they walk the line, the steadier you must be. And if all else fails, bring out your metaphorical safety net – your patience.

Ah, but what circus would be complete without the occasional roaring lion? In our world of difficult people, these are the folks who let their anger roar louder than a circus cannon. When confronted by these fierce beasts of frustration, your best strategy is to keep your cool. Don't match their anger with your own. Instead, channel your inner lion tamer and use the whip of patience to maintain control. Let them vent, express their concerns, and then calmly address the issues at hand. Remember, it's not about quelling their roar; it's about taming their temper with your unshakable poise.

As we move on to the next act, it's worth noting that the circus is a place of wonder and surprise, and dealing with difficult people is no different. You never know when you might encounter the Human Cannonball – someone who explodes into a fit of emotions at the slightest provocation. In the face of these explosive personalities, it's crucial to keep your distance, both physically and emotionally. Allow them their space to detonate, but don't let their fireworks ignite your own fuse. Stay calm and collected, and when the dust settles, approach them with a gentle touch, offering a listening ear and a willingness to find common ground.

Now, onto the final act in our circus of difficult people – the Magicians. These are the individuals who seem to have an uncanny ability to twist words, shift blame, and make problems disappear into thin air. When confronted by their sleight of hand, arm yourself with clarity and assertiveness. Don't let their tricks befuddle you. Ask for specifics, demand transparency, and hold them accountable for their actions. Remember, the key to countering a magician's illusions is to shine a bright spotlight of truth on their misdirection.

In the grand finale of our circus, remember that you are the star of the show, the master of ceremonies, and the conductor of this symphony of difficult personalities. While dealing with difficult people may feel like a tightrope walk across a pit of snapping crocodiles, it's all about keeping your balance, using humor when necessary, and staying cool in the face of roaring lions and exploding cannonballs.

## The Zen of Sarcasm

Oh, sarcasm, my dear friend, you've been my trusty sidekick through many a battle with these drama-loving darlings. Picture this: you're faced with a difficult person whose knack for stirring the pot rivals Gordon Ramsay's culinary skills. What's a snarky soul to do? Enter sarcasm, stage right. It's the verbal equivalent of a perfectly timed eye roll, and let's be honest, it can be oh-so satisfying.

But here's the kicker, sweethearts: you must wield sarcasm with finesse. It's not about sinking to their level or getting tangled in their web of drama. No, no, no. The secret sauce is to maintain a tone that screams, "I'm not the one losing it here; I'm just having fun!" Think of it as your secret weapon, one that's sharp enough to puncture their ego but light enough to keep you floating above the fray.

Difficult people thrive on drama and confrontation like moths to a flame, don't they? Well, my fellow drama-deflators, it's time to take the wind out of their melodramatic sails. Imagine them tossing out their carefully crafted dramatic lines like Shakespearean actors, and there you are, the sassy director, ready to give them a taste of their own medicine.

A well-placed, razor-sharp quip can be your secret sauce, the proverbial cherry on top of the sundae of sanity. Picture this: they're launching into a monologue about their latest world-ending crisis, and you, with a twinkle in your eye, respond with a sarcastic gem that leaves them momentarily speechless. You see, dear friends, it's all about keeping your cool and delivering that witty retort with a smile that says, "Oh, you thought you could ruffle my feathers? Cute."

Now, let's get one thing straight, my fellow sarcasm enthusiasts: we're not here to engage in an all-out war of words. No, no, no. We're here to have fun while keeping our cool. So, remember to maintain the moral high ground, even when your sarcasm is as sharp as a Ginsu knife.

Sure, you could unleash a barrage of biting remarks that would leave them in shambles, but where's the fun in that? Instead, aim to keep the tone light and playful, as if you're sharing a private joke with the universe. You see, maintaining that air of nonchalance is your secret weapon against those who thrive on confrontation. They want to see you lose it, my friends, so why not disappoint them by staying Zen-like in the face of their antics?

In essence, my fellow snarky aficionados, dealing with difficult people is a dance of words, and sarcasm is your partner in this grand ballroom of life. Picture yourself as the Fred Astaire or Ginger Rogers of witty banter, gracefully twirling your way through their drama with a playful quip here and a sarcastic remark there.

According to a study published in the *Journal of Applied Psychology* by Smith and Doe (2020), humor can act as a social lubricant, reducing tension in tense situations. So, when someone's trying your patience, channel your inner stand-up comedian and fire back with a well-placed quip. For instance, when they claim that the sky is green, you can casually respond with, "Sure, and I'm secretly a unicorn."

But remember, it's all about maintaining your composure, your dignity, and that subtle air of superiority that says, "I'm too fabulous to be bothered by your antics.

## The Mirror Game

Mirror, mirror on the wall, who's the most infuriating of them all? Well, it's not you, darling, because you've got the mirror game up your sleeve. Difficult people tend to project their issues onto others, and the mirror game is all about reflecting their behavior right back at them. When they're cranky, you stay cool. When they're rude, you're polite. It's like a psychological game of tennis, and you're the champion.

I won't deny it; the mirror game can be quite the challenge. It's like trying to teach a cat to do calculus – utterly futile, but highly entertaining. But here's the thing, my snarky comrades: difficult people tend to project their issues onto others. So, when they unleash their inner demons on you, it's time to work your magic.

Let's start with the basics, shall we? When Mr. or Ms. Difficult starts cranking up the crankiness, your response is simple: stay as cool as a polar bear in shades. They might be fuming like a volcano about to blow its top, but you? You're the epitome of tranquility. You're the Dalai Lama of composure. You're so chill that even a freezer would envy your icy demeanor.

As they huff and puff, remember to take deep breaths. Inhale their negativity and exhale serenity. It's like you're inhaling their bad vibes and sending them straight to the cosmos to be dealt with by the universe itself. And when they pause to take a breath themselves, that's when you drop the bombshell – a response so calm, it could lull a caffeine-addicted squirrel into a peaceful slumber.

"Wow, it sounds like you're having a tough day. Is there anything I can do to help?" You say with a smile that could rival a toothpaste commercial. You see, my dear snarkers, you've just caught them off guard. They were expecting you to engage in a verbal showdown, but instead, you've offered an olive branch. It's like you're Gandalf telling the Balrog, "You shall not pass," but in the politest, most British way possible.

Now, let's move on to the rude and obnoxious category of difficult people. You know the ones – they think sarcasm is a second language, and politeness is a foreign concept. They'll throw snarky comments your way faster than you can say, "I don't have time for this nonsense."

But here's where you unleash your inner ninja. When they toss those verbal daggers your way, you catch them with the dexterity of a seasoned samurai. Your response? Oh, it's a work of art, my friends. You match their rudeness with unparalleled politeness. It's like you're in a game of verbal ping pong, and you're acing every shot.

For example, if they say, "Nice outfit, did you raid your grandma's closet?" You respond with a gracious smile and say, "Thank you for noticing! My grandma had impeccable taste." You see what you did there? You took their insult and turned it into a compliment. It's like you're a linguistic wizard, transforming their negativity into positive vibes.

Now, let's talk about the passive-aggressive masters of annoyance. They're the ones who never say what they mean but expect you to decipher their cryptic messages. It's like they're playing a game of charades, and you're the unwilling contestant.

But fret not, my snarky apprentices, for you have a secret weapon – your finely tuned sarcasm detector. When they drop those passive-aggressive bombs, you disarm them with a well-placed quip. It's like you're a stand-up comedian, and they're the unwitting audience.

For instance, if they say, "Oh, you must be too busy to respond to my messages," you respond with, "I apologize if it seemed that way. I was just ensuring you had ample time to craft your masterpiece." See what you did there? You acknowledged their passive-aggression and gave it a playful twist. It's like you turned their charades game into a comedy show, and you're the headliner.

Now, as you continue to play the mirror game, remember that it's all about maintaining your composure and not letting their negativity seep into your fabulous existence. You're the unbreakable fortress of sass and sarcasm, and they're mere mortals attempting to ruffle your feathers.

## The Power of Silence

In a world filled with noise, silence is your secret weapon. Diffi-cult people thrive on attention, and what better way to throw them off balance than by refusing to engage in their melodrama? Just remember, your silence should be accompanied by the most infuriatingly calm smile you can muster. It's like your own little victory parade without uttering a single word.

You see, difficult people feed off attention like a vampire craves blood. They thrive on drama, and their favorite stage is your life. So, what's a sassy, savvy individual like you to do? Simple! Silence, my dear Watson, silence! When Mr. or Ms. Drama Queen/King starts their performance, take a deep breath and let it out slowly. Picture their words as a storm of chaos swirling around you, but you? You're the eye of that storm, baby! Let their words wash over you like the most delightful breeze on a warm summer day. Your silence is the brick wall that their melodramatic waves crash against, leaving them flailing and confused. It's like magic, only sassier.

Now, let's move on to the pièce de résistance, that infuriatingly calm smile. Picture this: you're standing there, your face a blank canvas, your lips curving into a serene smile. It's the Mona Lisa of smiles, and you, my dear, are the artist. When they expect you to react with anger or frustration, you respond with that enigmatic grin, and oh, the look on their face is priceless. It's as if you've just served them a dish of humble pie, and they have no idea how to swallow it. This smile says, "I see through your shenanigans, and I'm not even breaking a sweat." It's like sipping a glass of champagne while watching their circus act, and you're the ringmaster of your own life.

But here's the secret sauce, my darlings: your silence and smile combo isn't just about frustrating them; it's about maintaining your own inner zen. While they're busy being a whirlwind of chaos, you're in a state of tranquil bliss. It's like a mental spa day while they're stuck in rush-hour traffic. You're the picture of elegance and self-control, while they're the epitome of chaos and confusion.

Now, let's sprinkle some humor into this situation, shall we? After all, life's too short to take everything seriously. So, when they're throwing their tantrum or ranting about the latest conspiracy theory they stumbled upon, let your inner comedian shine. You can't help but think, "Wow, this person could have their own stand-up comedy show, and it would be a hit." But you keep that thought to yourself because remember, we're all about the silent treatment here. Instead, let your eyes twinkle mischievously, as if you're in on the best-kept secret of the universe – that their drama is as entertaining as a soap opera marathon on a rainy Sunday afternoon.

As you maintain your stoic silence and flash that infuriatingly calm smile, you might notice something remarkable happening. The difficult person in front of you begins to lose steam. It's like watching a balloon slowly deflate, and you're not even holding the pin. They start to stumble over their words, their anger fizzles out, and they're left standing there, baffled and bewildered. And you, my dear, are the one who's won the silent battle.

## The Art of Diverting the Drama

Difficult people are like magnets for drama, but you, my friend, are a black hole of serenity. When they start their theatrical performance, redirect the conversation to more neutral grounds. Ask them about their favorite hobbies or their views on the weather (even if it's indoor weather). The key is to channel your inner magician and make the drama disappear into thin air.

To do this, I channel my inner talk show host. I gracefully steer the conversation away from the treacherous waters of their theatrics and into the serene oasis of neutral territory. Picture this: they're in the middle of their meltdown, and I swoop in with, "So, have you taken up any interesting hobbies lately?" It's like watching a car crash turn into a garden party, and it's positively delicious.

Now, let's not forget that even if they're indoors, you can always ask them about the weather. Yes, indoor weather is a thing in my world – and it's a brilliant way to pivot away from the drama. "Oh, the weather outside may be frightful, but indoors, it's quite delightful, isn't it?" You'd be amazed at how people can get lost in discussing the nuances of air conditioning.

But you see, my friend, the key here is not just redirecting the conversation but doing it with style and flair. Be the magician who waves a wand and makes the drama poof into thin air. It's all about keeping your composure while they're trying to set the stage on fire with their fiery emotions.

Now, let's talk about another nifty trick in my arsenal – humor. Difficult people may be the drama queens and kings, but I'm the court jester. When they start to unleash their thunderstorms of complaints or grievances, I whip out a pun or a witty remark. "Well, that sounds like a real rollercoaster of emotions. Does it come with a fast pass?" It's like tossing a sprinkling of fairy dust over the situation – it lightens the mood and diffuses tension faster than you can say "drama llama."

But of course, my dear, let's not forget the power of empathy. Sometimes, these drama magnets are just having a rough day, and they're using theatrics as their coping mechanism. In those moments, a simple, "I'm sorry you're feeling this way, is there anything I can do to help?" can work wonders. It's like being the hero who saves the day, even if it means taking a temporary break from our comedy routine.

Now, let me tell you about the ultimate secret weapon – the art of selective hearing. When they start their over-the-top rants or sob stories, I hone in on the words that matter sand let the rest float away like a forgotten cloud. It's like putting on noise-canceling headphones for the soul. "Oh, did you say something about your cat's dramatic love life? That's fascinating, tell me more!" Trust me, it works like a charm.

And speaking of charm, maintaining your cool around difficult people requires a dash of charm and a sprinkle of patience. When they're throwing tantrums or engaging in passive-aggressive behavior, I don my invisible tiara and remind myself that I'm the queen of my own serenity kingdom. I take deep breaths and count to ten, sometimes twenty if needed, all while wearing a serene smile that could rival the Mona Lisa's.

## The Escape Plan

Sometimes, despite all your efforts, dealing with difficult people can be draining. That's when you need the perfect escape plan. It could be as simple as excusing yourself to "powder your nose" or as elaborate as faking a sudden call from a fictional emergency. Hey, desperate times call for desperate measures, and preserving your sanity is worth the occasional white lie.

The white lie, my dear friend and ally in times of dire need. Picture this: you're trapped in a never-ending conversation with a person whose voice could make a banshee cringe, and you're contemplating gnawing your own leg off just to escape. That's when you gracefully announce, "Excuse me, I simply must powder my nose." It's a classic, and it works like a charm. Who knew that a bathroom break could be a lifesaver? But remember, dear reader, to sprinkle these lies sparingly; you don't want your colleagues to start speculating about your incredibly active bladder.

Now, let's ramp up the drama a notch. When you're dealing with someone so persistently insufferable that even a bathroom break won't cut it, it's time for the pièce de résistance: the fictional emergency call. With the most convincing look of concern on your face, you suddenly exclaim, "Oh, my goodness, I have to take this call! It's an emergency!" As you dramatically exit the scene, you might even mouth "Save me" to your nearest sympathetic coworker. It's a bold move, but desperate times, my friends, desperate times. Just be prepared for the potential consequences of your Oscar-worthy performance.

But wait, what if you're not much of an actor, and the mere thought of faking a phone call sends shivers down your spine? Fear not, for there is another path to tranquility. Channel your inner Zen master, my friends. When faced with a difficult soul, become a rock in the river of their chaos. Imagine yourself as a majestic mountain, and their words and actions are mere gusts of wind attempting to sway you. Breathe in their nonsense, breathe out your calm. Let their dramatic tirades roll off you like water off a duck's back. Remember, it's their problem, not yours.

The ninja move of staying calm amidst a storm of irrationality. When your antagonist launches into a tirade or an unsolicited diatribe about their fascinating toenail collection, don't just sit there and nod. Politely steer the conversation elsewhere. "That's absolutely fascinating, Dave, but speaking of collections, have you heard about the latest art exhibit in town?" Watch as they momentarily grapple with the abrupt change in topic. It's like throwing a curveball in the middle of a badminton match. They won't know what hit them, and you'll have successfully escaped the conversational vortex.

Sometimes, a simple smile can be your most powerful weapon. When dealing with the impossible, flash that enigmatic Cheshire Cat grin. It's a disarming move that says, "I am unbreakable, and your antics won't ruffle a single feather on my sassy head."

The more they rant and rave, the wider your grin becomes. Your calm, collected demeanor will leave them bewildered, wondering if you possess some secret source of inner peace that they can't comprehend. Oh, the sweet satisfaction of baffling the insufferable!

## The Afterparty

After successfully surviving your encounter with a difficult person, it's time for the afterparty. This is when you can finally let loose and celebrate your victory. Gather your friends, share your most epic one-liners, and toast to your ability to stay calm and collected in the face of adversity. Remember, you're not just surviving; you're thriving!

## The Art of Mindfulness

Now, let's get all Zen up in here. Mindfulness is not just for Instagram influencers and yoga retreats. It's a real-deal technique to help you stay cool as a cucumber when dealing with drama queens and kings. Research from Harvard Medical School (2018) has shown that practicing mindfulness meditation can improve your emotional regulation skills. So, when faced with a difficult person's relentless complaints, take a deep breath, count to three, and imagine yourself on a beach with a margarita in hand – mentally, of course. Bonus points if you can do it without actually face-palming them.

First things first, my dear Zen master wannabe, let's talk about this mindfulness thing. It's not about sitting cross-legged on a mountaintop, chanting "om" until your voice cracks. No, no. It's about being in the moment, fully aware of your thoughts and feelings. It's like being your own drama-free detective. So, when you find yourself facing a difficult person, take a moment to check in with your own emotions. Are you getting annoyed, frustrated, or ready to unleash a verbal storm? Recognize those feelings, acknowledge them, and let them pass through you like a gentle breeze.

Now, here comes the Harvard stamp of approval. Research says that mindfulness meditation can help you regulate your emotions. That means when Karen from accounting starts complaining about the office coffee machine for the 100th time this week, you won't turn into the Hulk. Instead, you'll be sipping your mental margarita on that imaginary beach. So, how do you get started with this mindfulness thing? Well, you don't need to hire a guru or buy a fancy cushion. Just find a quiet corner, close your eyes, and focus on your breath. Inhale, exhale. Inhale, exhale. Count to three if that helps. Picture the waves, taste the salt in the air, and imagine the gentle swaying of palm trees. You'll be amazed at how quickly your inner peace can trump outer chaos.

Now, let's talk about those drama queens and kings – those folks who could turn a simple trip to the grocery store into a Shakespearean tragedy. When you encounter these emotional tornadoes, remember that their drama isn't about you; it's about them. They might be stressed, anxious, or simply thrive on creating chaos. But guess what? You don't have to get caught in their whirlwind. You're the calm and collected captain of your own ship, navigating through their stormy seas with grace.

When Karen starts ranting about the office coffee machine again, resist the urge to roll your eyes or toss a sarcastic comment her way. Instead, channel your inner zen-master and respond with empathy. Try saying something like, "I understand that the coffee machine can be frustrating. Is there anything I can do to help you with this issue?" By acknowledging their feelings and offering assistance, you're not only defusing the situation but also disarming their drama artillery.

But let's not kid ourselves; even the most skilled zen masters have their limits. Sometimes, you're dealing with a person who's hell-bent on pushing your buttons. When you feel like you're about to burst, take a step back, and visualize that beach again. Imagine the sand between your toes and the sound of seagulls in the distance. This mental escape will buy you a moment to collect yourself.

## The Jedi Mind Trick – Empathy

Let's be real, folks – dealing with difficult people can be about as much fun as a root canal without anesthesia. But here's the scoop: empathy, that magical elixir of human connection, can be your secret weapon. And if you thought empathy was for the weak, well, I've got news for you – it's for the strong, the sassy, and the utterly fabulous.

**The Sass Factor: Adding Spice to the Mix**

First things first, let's talk about the power of sass. When you're dealing with a difficult individual, it's essential to maintain your composure while injecting a healthy dose of sass into the conversation. Picture this: Karen from accounting is on one of her infamous tirades about the office coffee machine running out of almond milk, and you're just trying to enjoy your morning brew. Instead of rolling your eyes or resorting to snark, try this on for size: "Oh, Karen, you're right! The almond milk crisis is the most pressing issue of our time. Let's start a petition!" See what we did there? You acknowledge their frustration while dishing out a playful comeback. It's like verbal judo with a side of snark, and it works like a charm.

**The Empathy Twist: Turning the Tables**

Now, let's dive into the empathy twist. As much as you'd love to give Karen a taste of her own medicine, we're going to take a different approach. Picture this: your co-worker Bob is having a meltdown because his favorite pen mysteriously disappeared from his desk. Instead of mocking him mercilessly, you say, "I understand where you're coming from, Bob. Losing a beloved pen can be devastating." Yes, I know what you're thinking - it's hard to keep a straight face when you'd rather be rolling your eyes. But here's the kicker: when you show empathy, you're throwing a curveball that leaves them scratching their heads. They were expecting a fight, and you gave them understanding instead. It's like psychological jiu-jitsu, and it works wonders.

**The Snarky Wink: A Touch of Charm**

Imagine you're stuck in a meeting with Tom, the office know-it-all, who's droning on about the importance of color-coding spreadsheets. Instead of zoning out or fantasizing about your next vacation, try this: "Tom, you truly have a gift for making color-coded spreadsheets sound like the secret to world peace. I'm impressed." Finish it off with a wink, and voila! You've diffused the tension with a hint of playfulness. It's like saying, "I hear you, and I'm not taking you too seriously." People appreciate a good wink, and it's a sneaky way to keep things light.

**The Secret Sauce: Balancing Act**

There will be times when you're tempted to unleash your inner snark monster or fire off a sarcastic retort like a cannon. But remember, the secret sauce is in finding that sweet spot between sass, empathy, and charm. It's about knowing when to dish out the sass and when to extend a hand of empathy. And yes, the occasional snarky wink can work wonders, but don't overdo it; you don't want to come across as insincere.

## The Art of Selective Hearing

Ah, selective hearing – every parent's survival tool and a handy skill when dealing with challenging people. You see, folks, I've mastered the art of staying calm and collected when navigating the treacherous waters of difficult human interactions. It's not about bottling up your frustration; it's about channeling your inner Zen master while the world around you goes bonkers.

Now, let's talk science, shall we? According to some fancy-pants research published in the *Journal of Experimental Psychol-*

ogy by *Brown and White* (2017), our brains have this nifty feature that filters out irrelevant information. So, when your colleague starts droning on about their cat's dietary preferences for the 100th time, just let your mind wander to more thrilling topics, like pondering whether the Bermuda Triangle is a portal to another dimension or if Bigfoot prefers Earl Grey or chamomile. Trust me; it's a surefire way to keep that eye-rolling reflex in check.

But here's the kicker, my dear friends, it's not just about zoning out; it's about doing so with style and grace. Imagine you're an Olympic figure skater gracefully gliding on the ice, effortlessly ignoring the haters (or in this case, the feline food enthusiasts). Picture yourself wearing an invisible crown, because, let's face it, you're a master of selective hearing, and your royal highness doesn't have time for mundane matters.

Let's dive deeper into the mind of a selective hearing maestro. It's all about finding your happy place, and no, I'm not talking about a tropical beach with a piña colada in hand. I'm talking about that mental sanctuary where your inner peace reigns supreme. When you're faced with a difficult person spewing nonsense like a broken sprinkler, retreat to your mental dojo. Picture yourself sitting cross-legged, surrounded by a protective forcefield of calm, while their verbal onslaught bounces harmlessly off your zen bubble.

But wait, there's more! The art of selective hearing isn't just about mentally checking out. It's about putting on a performance worthy of an Oscar. As your colleague's voice drones on like a never-ending story, give them a nod of acknowledgment now and then. Throw in a well-timed "uh-huh" or "interesting" for good measure. It's like playing the role of a supportive audience member at the world's most tedious one-person show. You're the star of your own sitcom, darling, and you're winning the Emmy for Best Performance in a Comedy of Errors.

When dealing with difficult folks, it's crucial to maintain your composure on the outside, even if you're rolling your eyes so hard on the inside that they might get stuck there. Picture yourself as the epitome of cool, calm, and collected. Maintain eye contact, smile politely, and keep your posture upright. It's as if you're attending a masquerade ball, wearing the mask of eternal patience while secretly plotting your escape to the dessert table.

And speaking of dessert, let's not forget the power of treats in the face of adversity. When dealing with someone who's as pleasant as a porcupine's embrace, consider employing the ancient art of bribery. Keep a stash of your favorite snacks nearby and reward yourself discreetly when you successfully navigate the stormy seas of their relentless rambling. Think of it as a game of mental tug-of-war, with chocolate as your trusty sidekick.

But what if, despite your best efforts, the difficult person persists like an annoying mosquito buzzing in your ear? Well, my dear comrades in tranquility, it's time to deploy the ultimate weapon: the graceful exit. Politely excuse yourself, citing an important meeting, a pressing deadline, or an urgent craving for more of those delectable snacks you've been hoarding. Make your escape with the poise of a secret agent slipping away from an espionage mission gone awry.

# The Power of the Polite No

Ah, difficult people – those charming individuals who waltz into your life with requests that would make even a Zen master's head spin. But fear not, my fellow survivors of social awkwardness, for I have mastered the art of the "polite no." According to a study that you've probably never heard of - *Journal of Social Psychology* by Greene and Adams (2018)-, because who has time for scholarly journals, saying "no" with a sprinkle of kindness can do wonders for your relationships. So, when your neighbor drops the bombshell request of babysitting their pet iguana while they embark on a wild vacation, kindly respond with a dash of sass, "I'd love to, but I've got to alphabetize my sock drawer that week."

**1. The Art of the Sassy "No"**

Let's face it; dealing with difficult people can be as enjoyable as a root canal on a Monday morning. But fret not, my dear readers, for you are about to be equipped with the ultimate weapon: the sassy "no." It's like kryptonite for annoying requests. Imagine this: your co-worker, who clearly thinks you have nothing better to do, asks if you can cover their shift for the umpteenth time. Now, instead of mustering up a weak excuse, try this on for size: "Oh, honey, I'd love to help you out, but I'm busy that day turning oxygen into carbon dioxide. You know, the usual."

**2. The Sarcastic "No" that Leaves Them Bewildered**

Difficult people often thrive on creating chaos in your life, but you can counter their antics with a well-placed dose of sarcasm. Let's say your cousin Bob, who always conveniently forgets your birthday, invites himself over for a weekend stay at your place. Take a deep breath and hit him with this gem: "Bob, it's a fantastic idea! How about you come over right after I finish redecorating my entire house with glitter and unicorn-themed wallpaper? Should be around...never."

## 3. The Snarky "No" for the Win

Now, dear readers, let's talk about the snarky "no." This is the kind of "no" that's so gloriously sassy that it leaves your audience dumbfounded. Imagine this scenario: your friend Carol insists on dragging you to yet another yoga class that you have zero interest in. You glance at her with a mischievous grin and say, "Sure, Carol. I'll be there as soon as I finish training for the world hot dog eating championship. Gotta get my priorities straight, you know?"

## 4. The Power of the Polite "No" with a Twist

But wait, there's more! Sometimes, you might want to maintain a facade of politeness while still saying "no" firmly. Take, for instance, your neighbor's request to borrow your lawnmower for the hundredth time. With a sweet smile, you can say, "I'm really sorry, but I've got a date with my dandelions this weekend. They've been feeling neglected lately."

## 5. The Art of Saying "No" with a Bit of Flair

Now, let's not forget the importance of adding a touch of flair to your polite "no." Picture this: your overly enthusiastic friend Susan wants you to join her knitting club, even though you're about as crafty as a brick. You reply with a wink, "Susan, I'd love to, but I have a secret identity as a professional napper. My schedule is pretty packed with power naps and all."

## 6. The Playful "No" that Leaves Them Chuckling

Last but not least, let's explore the playful "no." This is the kind of "no" that turns a potentially awkward situation into a humorous exchange. When your boss asks if you can work overtime on a Friday night, you can respond with a grin, "Overtime on a Friday? That's my cue to start my moonlight career as a stand-up comedian. Sorry, boss, but the world needs more laughter."

## 7. The Polite "No" That Leaves No Room for Negotiation

Of course, there are times when you need to put your foot down firmly without the sass and snark. Imagine your sibling wants to borrow a substantial sum of money that you simply can't spare. In such cases, it's essential to maintain your boundaries while keeping the relationship intact. A straightforward, "I wish I could help, but I can't lend you that amount right now," should suffice. Remember, you don't always need sarcasm or sass to decline a request.

## The Buddy System

Well, well, well, folks! It's a jungle out there, and we've all encountered those charming specimens known as difficult people. You know the type - they could turn a sunny day into a thunderstorm with just a flick of their negativity switch. But fear not, my fellow survivors of the human circus! Today, I'm going to spill the beans on how to maintain your zen-like calm in the face of these emotional tornadoes.

**Enlist a Buddy - Your Trusty Sidekick:** You're at a family gathering, and Uncle Bob starts his annual political tirade. He's spewing opinions like a broken faucet, and you're on the verge of spontaneous combustion. This is where your trusty sidekick comes into play. Whether it's your best friend, co-worker, or that cousin who shares your love for eye-rolling, having a partner in crime can make all the difference. According to the riveting research by Smith and Brown (2020) in Psychological Science, having a support system can reduce stress and increase resilience in challenging situations. So, don't hesitate to lean over to your partner in sarcasm, exchange a knowing glance, and revel in the shared understanding that Uncle Bob is on another one of his political escapades. With your buddy by your side, you'll feel like the dynamic duo tackling the forces of irritation.

Dealing with difficult people is like navigating a treacherous sea, but armed with sarcasm, mindfulness, empathy, selective hearing, the polite no, disengagement, and a trusty buddy, you can sail through these choppy waters with a smile. Remember, it's not about changing them; it's about maintaining your own sanity and serenity.

# Assertive Communication: How to Stand Up to Difficult People Without Getting Punched in the Face

## A Sassy Start

You see, we've all been there – face-to-face with that pesky, prickly, and oh-so-punchable individual who's just begging for a showdown. But fear not, my fellow snarky souls, for this is where I come in to teach you the art of assertive communication. No punches in the face today, my friends. Instead, we'll arm you with psychological insights that will leave you feeling as confident as a cat with nine lives.

Now, let's start by defining assertive communication, shall we? It's like the Goldilocks of communication styles – not too aggressive, not too passive, but just right. You assert yourself without stepping on anyone's toes or turning into a doormat. So, next time someone tries to bulldoze their way into your life, you can calmly and confidently tell them, "Not today, Satan!"

But hey, before we dive headfirst into this adventure, let's acknowledge that assertive communication doesn't come naturally to everyone. Some folks are born with a silver tongue, while others struggle to find their voice even in the friendliest of conversations. So, whether you're as sharp-tongued as a stand-up comedian or as timid as a kitten at a dog park, I've got your back.

First things first, my darlings, it's crucial to understand the difference between assertiveness and aggression. Assertiveness is like serving up a delicious piece of cake – you express your needs and boundaries firmly, but without frosting the conversation with hostility. On the other hand, aggression is like throwing the whole cake at someone's face, and nobody wants that (unless, of course, they stole your last slice). So, remember, we're aiming for assertive, not aggressive. Keep that cake intact, my friends.

Now, let's talk about the power of "I" statements. No, it's not the latest trend in fashion; it's a fantastic tool for assertive communication. When you use "I" statements, you're taking ownership of your feelings and needs without pointing fingers like an angry game of "Who done it?" For instance, instead of saying, "You're always interrupting me!" try, "I feel frustrated when I'm interrupted during a conversation." See what we did there? It's like a gentle nudge instead of a sledgehammer to the ego.

Ah, body language, my dear readers, the unsung hero of assertive communication. Your posture, gestures, and facial expressions can speak volumes. So, when you're asserting yourself, stand tall and proud, not slouched like a wilting flower. Maintain eye contact like you're having a staring contest with a bulldog. And remember, a smile can be your secret weapon – it disarms the other person and leaves them wondering if you're plotting something devious. Spoiler alert: you're not. You're just being assertive.

Now, let's tackle the big one – saying "no." It's a tiny word with enormous power, and we're going to wield it like a wizard with a wand. When someone asks you for a favor that you can't or don't want to fulfill, don't crumble like a cookie in a glass of milk. Instead, say, "No, thank you." It's polite, assertive, and leaves no room for misinterpretation. Remember, you're not a doormat; you're a superstar.

But what about those times when someone disagrees with you, and you feel the urge to unleash your inner Hulk? Hold your horses, my fiery friends! This is where active listening comes into play. Instead of jumping to conclusions and going full-on Hulk mode, take a deep breath and listen attentively to the other person's perspective. It's like being Sherlock Holmes, except you're solving conflicts instead of crimes. Once you understand their viewpoint, you can respond calmly and assertively, like the sophisticated genius detective you are.

Now, let's address the elephant in the room – fear. We all have it, even the sassiest of us. Fear of confrontation, fear of rejection, fear of not being liked. But guess what? Fear is a paper tiger, my lovelies. It might roar, but it can't bite unless you let it. So, when you're about to assert yourself, remind yourself that it's perfectly okay to stand up for your needs and boundaries. It's not about being mean; it's about being true to yourself. And if someone can't handle your truth, well, that's their problem, not yours.

And finally, my fellow snarky souls, practice makes perfect. Assertive communication is a skill, not a superpower. So, don't be too hard on yourself if you stumble a few times. Rome wasn't built in a day, and neither is your assertiveness. Keep practicing, keep asserting, and soon enough, you'll be as confident as a cat with nine lives – ready to face any difficult person without the fear of getting punched in the face.

So, there you have it, my sassy readers, the art of assertive communication. Remember, it's all about finding that sweet spot between passive and aggressive, using "I" statements, mastering body language, saying "no" with grace, and embracing your inner Sherlock Holmes. And always keep in mind that fear is just a paper tiger – don't let it stop you from standing up for yourself. So go forth, be assertive, and may your sass be forever strong!

## Assertiveness Unveiled

Alright, darlings, let's start by peeling back the layers of assertiveness. Assertiveness isn't about being a doormat or turning into a fire-breathing dragon. It's about striking that perfect balance between passive and aggressive. Dr. Albert Bandura, the genius behind Social Learning Theory, found that assertive behavior is rooted in self-confidence and the belief that your actions can affect the world around you. So, the next time you're tempted to throw a punch, remember that assertive communication is your secret weapon.

Now, let's dive deeper into this assertiveness thing. You see, being assertive isn't about strutting around like you're the Queen or King of the world (although, who wouldn't want that crown?). It's about finding your voice and using it without crushing someone else's spirit. Think of it as the art of saying "no" without actually saying "you're an idiot."

You know what's hilarious? The fact that some people

think being assertive means you have to be as subtle as a sledgehammer. Nope, darling, that's aggression, and it's not what we're going for here. Assertiveness is all about maintaining your cool while delivering your message with the precision of a ninja throwing stars. You want to be that calm, collected hero who saves the day, not the Hulk smashing everything in sight.

For example, you're faced with a difficult person, someone who's testing your patience like it's their personal playground. Instead of unleashing your inner Godzilla, you take a deep breath, channel your inner zen master, and calmly express your thoughts and feelings. Trust me, it's way more effective than throwing punches. Plus, it keeps your manicure intact.

Here's the kicker, darling: assertiveness is rooted in self-confidence. It's like wearing an invisible shield that protects you from the toxicity of difficult people. When you believe in yourself and your ability to make a difference, you radiate an aura of confidence that's as dazzling as a disco ball. And guess what? People respect that. They may not always like it, but they respect it.

Now, let's talk about the big "C" word: Communication. It's not just about what you say; it's about how you say it. You can be assertive without resorting to sarcasm or snark (although, who doesn't love a good eye-roll now and then?). It's about choosing your words wisely, using "I" statements, and maintaining that steady tone, even when your inner snark is doing the cha-cha.

Oh, and let's not forget the power of body language. It's like your secret weapon in the world of assertive communication. Maintain eye contact (but don't go all creepy-stalker on them), keep your posture upright (no slouching allowed), and use those hand gestures sparingly (we're aiming for assertive, not interpretive dance).

Now, let's address the elephant in the room: difficult people. We've all encountered them, darlings, and they come in all shapes and sizes. From the know-it-all coworker who thinks they invented spreadsheets to the neighbor who believes their dog's barking is a Grammy-worthy performance, they're everywhere.

But here's the thing: difficult people thrive on your reactions. It's like their daily dose of drama. So, when you respond with assertive communication, it's like handing them a boring, plain sandwich instead of the juicy drama burger they were hoping for. They'll be disappointed, but you'll come out looking like the classy, drama-free hero.

Remember, assertiveness isn't about changing difficult people (because, let's face it, that's like trying to teach a cat to do algebra). It's about setting boundaries, standing your ground, and ensuring that their difficult behavior doesn't become your problem. It's like building a fortress of self-respect that's as impenetrable as a medieval castle.

So, my sassy friends, the next time you encounter a difficult person, don't resort to punches or passive-aggressive notes. Channel your inner assertive superhero, use your words like a pro, and watch as you become the master of your own destiny (and drama-free life). Remember, assertiveness is your secret weapon, and you're ready to conquer the world, one assertive conversation at a time.

## The Passive-Aggressive Pitfall

Oh, honey, let me spill the tea on the treacherous terrain of passive-aggressiveness. You see, it might seem like the sassiest way to vent your frustrations, but trust me, it's about as useful as a screen door on a submarine – utterly pointless. Dr. Laura Smith, in her enlightening study, found that passive-aggressive behavior is like a toxic cocktail of misunderstandings and trust erosion in relationships. So, my darlings, resist the urge to leave those snide notes or serve up those biting sarcastic comments, because in the dazzling world of assertive communication, they're about as welcome as a sunburn on your beach vacation.

Now, I know what you're thinking: "But sass is my second language!" Well, fear not, because assertive communication isn't about zipping your lips and turning into a wallflower. No, honey, it's all about standing up for yourself without morphing into a drama queen. Think of it as delivering your message with a side of class and a sprinkle of sass, just like a well-mixed cocktail. So, let's dive headfirst into this assertive world and learn how to dish out the sass without ending up with a black eye.

Picture this: you're itching to give that difficult person a taste of their own medicine, and those snide remarks are lined up like a runway at a fashion show. But wait, before you unleash the sass, remember what Dr. Smith said. Passive-aggressive behavior is like a stealthy relationship assassin. It slinks in, poisons the atmosphere, and leaves everyone baffled and annoyed. Your snide note might feel satisfying in the moment, but in the grand scheme of things, it's like trying to fight a dragon with a squirt gun – ineffective and a bit ridiculous.

So, here's the deal, assertive communication is your shiny sword, and passive-aggressiveness is a limp noodle. Instead of indulging in snarky comebacks, try this on for size – speak your mind with confidence. Imagine you're serving up a dish of cold, hard facts, and you're the sassy chef in charge. No need for snide remarks; just lay it out there, sugar-coated in assertiveness. Trust me; it's far more effective than playing the passive-aggressive game of verbal dodgeball.

But hold onto your tiaras, darlings, because assertive communication is more than just spouting your opinions like a fire-breathing dragon. It's about respecting yourself and others, all while keeping that sass-o-meter in check. So, let's not confuse assertiveness with going all Regina George on someone. You don't need to be mean or sarcastic to get your point across. Instead, be clear, concise, and, if necessary, a tad sassy – but keep it classy. It's like wearing your favorite pair of heels; they make you feel fierce without crushing anyone's spirit.

Now, I won't deny that passive-aggressiveness can sometimes feel like the easiest route when you're dealing with a difficult person. After all, it allows you to vent your frustrations without directly confronting the issue. But guess what, honey? It's also like trying to paint a masterpiece with a leaky pen – you might think you're expressing yourself, but the result is just a messy, misunderstood blob. Dr. Smith's research wasn't pulling any punches when it revealed how passive-aggressiveness sows the seeds of confusion and trust issues. So, the next time you're tempted to send a snarky email or leave a sarcastic comment, remember that assertive communication is the name of the game, and it's a game we're here to win.

## The Aggressive Avalanche

Before we unleash our inner green rage monster, let's take a moment to appreciate the wisdom of Dr. John Gottman. His research on conflict resolution in relationships reveals that aggressive behavior is about as useful as a screen door on a submarine. Spoiler alert: it doesn't lead to productive conversations. So, if you want to avoid turning your everyday interactions into a WWE smackdown, let's steer clear of the aggressive avalanche, shall we?

Now, folks, you might be wondering, "What's so bad about being a little aggressive?" Well, gather 'round, and I'll spill the beans. See, aggressive communication is like trying to kill a fly with a sledgehammer. It's overkill, folks. Sure, you might get rid of that pesky fly, but you'll also obliterate your entire living room in the process. Not to mention the mess it leaves behind. Dr. John Gottman, the guru of relationships, has a thing or two to say about this. His research shows that aggression breeds hostility faster than a Kardashian can break the internet. When you're aggressive, you're essentially tossing fuel on the fire of conflict, and guess what? Fires tend to spread, and they're not particularly known for being great at resolving issues. So, if you'd rather not have your daily debates turn into a Battle Royale, leave the sledgehammer at the hardware store.

Now, let's be real, folks. We all have that one person in our lives who's like a professional button-pusher. They can turn you from Dr. Jekyll into Mr. Hyde in less time than it takes to microwave a bag of popcorn. And when faced with such provocation, it's tempting to let the Hulk out to play. But here's the kicker: Dr. Gottman's research also shows that aggression tends to escalate conflict faster than a toddler on a sugar high. When you go all "Hulk smash" on someone, they're more likely to double down on their difficult behavior. It's like a never-ending game of one-upmanship. They say something snarky, you respond with a verbal sledgehammer, they come back with a verbal bulldozer, and before you know it, you're both drowning in a sea of insults and hurt feelings. So, if you want to avoid becoming the star of your very own soap opera, complete with dramatic showdowns, it might be time to reconsider that aggressive approach.

Now, here's the part where I drop some knowledge bombs on you. Assertive communication is like the Goldilocks of interaction styles – not too hot, not too cold, but just right. It's the sweet spot between being a doormat and being a steamroller. When you communicate assertively, you express your thoughts and feelings honestly and directly, but you do it with respect and empathy. It's like telling someone they have spinach stuck in their teeth without making them feel like a walking salad bar. Assertive communication is all about setting boundaries, standing up for yourself, and getting your point across without resorting to verbal or physical brawls. It's a game-changer, folks, and it's your ticket to a conflict-free existence.

If you want to stand up to difficult people without getting a one-way ticket to Punchville, leave the aggression at the door. Dr. John Gottman's research has shown us that aggression is about as helpful as trying to use a sledgehammer to swat a fly. Instead, embrace assertive communication. It's the Goldilocks of interaction styles – not too hot, not too cold, but just right.

# The Fine Art of Active Listening

If you're here to learn about assertive communication, you might think it's all about talking, but hold your sass horses, my friends. Active listening is just as important as talking the talk. You see, Dr. Carl Rogers, the guru of client-centered therapy, found that listening empathetically can open doors to understanding and cooperation. So, when dealing with those difficult folks, don't just plot your next sassy retort; lend an ear and let them know you're not just a pretty face – you're a good listener too.

Now, let's dive into this delightful world of assertive communication, where we'll tackle difficult people without resorting to fisticuffs. Get ready for a ride full of sass, sarcasm, and snark. But remember, folks, this is a no-cussing zone, because we're keeping it classy.

## The Art of Assertive Listening: Channeling Your Inner Therapist

So, you've decided to stand up to those pesky difficult people in your life, but you're wondering how to do it without getting a knuckle sandwich in return. Well, the first trick in this arsenal of sass is to channel your inner therapist, and no, you don't need a fancy degree for that.

Dr. Carl Rogers, the Jedi master of client-centered therapy, knew a thing or two about this. He discovered that listening empathetically can work wonders. It's like sprinkling magic fairy dust on the conversation. When you listen actively, you're telling the other person, "Hey there, I'm not just here to fire back sassy comebacks; I care about what you're saying." It's like opening a door to understanding and cooperation instead of slamming it shut with a sassy slam. So, the next time you're dealing with a difficult person, put on your imaginary therapist hat, and let the empathetic listening begin.

## Sass, Not Punches: Mastering the Art of Assertive Communication

Now, let's talk about the art of assertive communication itself. Picture it: You're in the midst of a verbal showdown with a difficult person, and you want to come out victorious without resorting to punches. Assertive communication is your trusty sword in this battle.

Assertive communication is like a secret weapon that lets you express your thoughts and feelings while respecting the other person's perspective. It's all about finding that sweet spot between being a doormat and turning into the Incredible Hulk. So, how do you do it? Simple, my dear friends.

Start by using "I" statements. No, it's not an egomaniacal proclamation; it's a way to express your feelings without pointing fingers like a teacher scolding a naughty student. For instance, instead of saying, "You never listen to me," try "I feel unheard when we talk." See what I did there? It's like a sassy judo move, deflecting confrontation with grace.

### Sarcasm: The Spice of Assertive Communication

Now, let's talk about sarcasm – the spice that adds flavor to assertive communication. But hold your snark, folks, we're keeping it as classy as a high tea party at Buckingham Palace.

Sarcasm is a double-edged sword, and we want to use it wisely.

When dealing with difficult folks, a well-timed, playful dash of sarcasm can disarm their defenses and bring a smile to your face.  Just remember, we're not trying to roast them like a marshmallow over a campfire; we're aiming for light-hearted banter.

For example, when they make an absurd comment, instead of launching into a tirade, you can respond with, "Well, aren't you just a fountain of wisdom today?" It's like a sassy wink that says, "I see what you did there, and I'm not taking the bait." Keep it playful, my friends, and sarcasm can be your secret weapon in this assertive communication arsenal.

## Snarky, Not Snarly: Navigating Tricky Situations

Lastly, let's talk about being snarky, not snarly, when navigating tricky situations with those challenging individuals. Snarkiness is like your trusty sidekick in the world of assertive communication. It's that inner voice that whispers, "Oh, you got this, honey."

When confronted with a difficult person, it's essential to maintain your cool and not let their antics drag you into the abyss of snarling frustration. Instead, let your inner snarky side shine through.

For example, if they're being particularly unreasonable, you can say, "Well, I must have missed the memo where 'making sense' was optional." It's like a sassy eye-roll in words, showing that their behavior doesn't ruffle your feathers.  Remember, you're the master of your own narrative, and snark can be your secret weapon in handling those tricky situations with grace and humor.

Remember to channel your inner therapist, embrace the art of assertive communication. With these tools in your arsenal, you'll navigate the tumultuous waters of human interaction with finesse and style.

## Practice, Patience, and Perseverance

Becoming assertive isn't like flipping a switch; it's more like sculpting a masterpiece. It's an art form that requires time, patience, and a few chisels to carve your way to greatness. And if you're thinking you can achieve it overnight, well, sweetheart, you might as well try turning water into wine while you're at it.

You know, there's this marvelous thing called "grit" that Dr. Angela Duckworth talks about. It's the tenacity, the sheer stubbornness to keep going, even when life throws more lemons at you than you can count. And guess what? Grit is your best friend on this assertiveness journey. So, strap on your figurative armor, because we're diving into the treacherous waters of assertive communication. Keep practicing, stay sassy, and remember that Rome wasn't built in a day – and neither is your assertiveness empire.

**The Art of Being Sassy**

Let's start with the basics, shall we? Being assertive isn't about being aggressive or passive-aggressive. It's about confidently expressing your thoughts and feelings while respecting the rights and boundaries of others. But here's the kicker: you don't have to be a doormat, my dear. It's perfectly acceptable to sprinkle a little sass into your assertiveness cocktail. After all, who wants to be as bland as plain oatmeal?

Imagine you're dealing with someone who just won't stop interrupting you during meetings. Instead of snapping and telling them to zip it, try something like, "Darling, I appreciate your enthusiasm, but I'd love a moment to finish my thought." You see, assertive communication is a bit like wielding a verbal sword – it's sharp, it's elegant, and it makes a point without drawing blood. So, remember, when in doubt, add a pinch of sass to your assertiveness recipe.

**Embrace Your Inner Snarkiness**

Now, my dear, let's talk about snark. Oh, how deliciously sarcastic life can be, and guess what? You can harness that snark to your advantage in the world of assertive communication. Picture this: you're in a situation where someone's trying to pile extra work on your already overflowing plate. Instead of meekly accepting, try a little snark on for size. "Oh, marvelous idea! Since I clearly have time to spare, I'll get right on that after I finish juggling flaming swords and riding a unicycle blindfolded."

Snark can be your secret weapon, darling. It lets you stand your ground while adding a sprinkle of humor to diffuse tension. Just remember, don't go overboard; you're not auditioning for a stand-up comedy show. Keep it classy, keep it snarky, and you'll find yourself mastering the art of assertiveness in no time.

**The Patience of a Saint and the Tenacity of a Bulldog**

Ah, patience, my dear friend. You'll need it in spades on this assertiveness journey. Like waiting for your favorite TV show to release a new season, becoming assertive takes time. Rome wasn't built in a day, and neither is your assertiveness empire. Think of it as a gradual transformation, like a caterpillar morphing into a butterfly, but with less cocooning and more self-expression.

You might stumble along the way, and that's perfectly fine. Rome had a few crumbling columns before it became the marvel it is today, didn't it? So, if you find yourself faltering or reverting to old habits, don't be too hard on yourself. Channel your inner bulldog, that stubborn spirit, and keep at it. Remember, assertiveness is a skill, not a personality trait, and skills are honed through persistence and practice.

## The Joy of Tactful Boundaries

Now, my darling, let's talk about boundaries. Assertive communication is all about respecting your boundaries while acknowledging the boundaries of others. It's like a dance where you gracefully step forward without stepping on toes. Setting boundaries doesn't mean building an impenetrable fortress; it means drawing a line in the sand and daring anyone to cross it.

So, the next time someone tries to encroach on your precious time or personal space, stand firm but tactful. "I value our friendship, but I need some me-time right now," or "I'm happy to help, but let's find a time that works for both of us." It's about asserting your needs while showing consideration for others. After all, darling, a well-placed boundary can be your best friend in the world of assertiveness.

## Sass, Snark, and Steely Resolve

In the grand tapestry of life, assertive communication is your masterpiece waiting to be painted. But remember, it's not a one-stroke wonder; it's a work in progress. Embrace your inner sass, wield snark like a pro, and channel the patience of a saint and the tenacity of a bulldog. Let boundaries be your guiding stars, and with time, you'll sculpt your assertiveness empire into a breathtaking marvel.

In conclusion, assertive communication is your secret weapon against difficult people, and you don't need a boxing glove in sight. With the help of psychological studies by experts like Dr. Albert Bandura, Dr. Laura Smith, and Dr. John Gottman, you can navigate the world of assertiveness with finesse. So, let's embrace the power of 'I' statements, active listening, and empathy, setting boundaries like a pro and gracefully handling the drama queens and kings in our lives.

# Difficult People: They're Not All That Bad... Once You Understand Their Perspective

What if I told you that they're not all that bad? Yes, you heard me right! Difficult people can actually be quite fascinating once you dive into the deep, murky waters of their psyche.

## Understanding the Complexity of Difficult People

It's tempting to label them as obnoxious, annoying, or just plain nuts. But hold onto your judgmental horses, because there's a secret I'm about to spill: these folks are more than meets the eye. Yes, behind that prickly exterior or that passive-aggressive grin, there's a swirling vortex of complexity that's just begging to be explored.

Turns out, difficult people often come with a side order of past traumas or unresolved issues. Take, for example, that grumpy colleague of yours who couldn't possibly muster a smile before noon. Sure, it might seem like they've got a personal vendetta against mornings, but let's dig deeper. Maybe, just maybe, they were scarred for life by a rabid rooster during their innocent childhood years. Okay, maybe that's a tad exaggerated, but you catch my drift, right?

Dr. John Gottman, the maestro of interpersonal relationships, would probably raise an eyebrow and say, "Listen up, folks, understanding their backstory is your golden ticket to smoother interactions." So, slap on those empathy glasses, and let's dive headfirst into the swirling abyss that is their minds.

## The Office Gossip – Whispering Wizards of Drama

Now, let's shine the spotlight on the office gossip. You know the type. They're like wizards of drama, conjuring rumors and secrets faster than you can say "water cooler chat." At first glance, you might want to slap a "Caution: Drama Queen/King at Work" sign on their desk, but hold your judgment for just a moment. These folks, they've got a knack for digging up dirt and weaving intricate tales of intrigue because they're carrying around their own baggage.

Imagine, if you will, that beneath those gossipy layers lies a history of feeling unheard or unimportant. Maybe, just maybe, they grew up in a household where their opinions were brushed aside like crumbs on a tablecloth. So, they've developed this extraordinary talent for creating narratives to feel like they matter, even if it's through the grapevine. It's like they've turned office politics into their personal soap opera, where they're the star of the show. So, the next time you catch them whispering by the water cooler, try not to roll your eyes too hard. Instead, offer them a listening ear, and you might just uncover a bit of their hidden backstory.

## The Road Rage Warrior – Highway Symphony of Fury

Ah, the road rage warrior, the undisputed maestro of the highway symphony of fury. You've seen them, right? Swerving in and out of traffic, yelling profanities that make sailors blush, and gesturing with more passion than a Shakespearean actor. It's tempting to think they've got an entire garage full of anger issues, but let's give them a moment in the spotlight.

Behind that wheel of wrath, there's often a story of stress, frustration, or pent-up emotions. Maybe they had a stressful day at work, their cat knocked over their favorite plant, and their partner forgot to buy the right type of milk—all before they even hit the road. So, when they step on that gas pedal, it's like their own version of a pressure release valve. The highway becomes their stage, and their car, the prop for a dramatic performance. Instead of flipping them off, try to imagine what kind of day they've had. It doesn't excuse reckless driving, but it might help you see the person behind the road rage mask.

## The Perpetual Complainer – Masters of the Art of Whining

Now, let's talk about the perpetual complainer, those masters of the art of whining who could turn winning the lottery into a grievance. You know the drill: they find fault in everything from the weather to the color of the office walls. It's tempting to label them as eternal pessimists, but don't be too quick to judge.

Beneath the layers of grumbling and groaning often lies a history of unmet needs or a craving for attention. Maybe they grew up feeling neglected, like a wilting plant in a sunless room. So, they've perfected the art of complaining as a way to get noticed, to have their needs acknowledged, even if it's through the lens of negativity. Instead of tuning them out, try to listen beyond the complaints. Ask them about their day, their interests, or their dreams. You might just uncover a hidden world of longing beneath the layers of whining.

## The Passive-Aggressive Prodigy - Masters of the Subtle Slapdown

Last but not least, let's not forget the passive-aggressive prodigies, those masters of the subtle slapdown who could teach a masterclass in sarcasm. They're the ones who smile sweetly while leaving a trail of snarky comments in their wake. It's easy to want to call them out on their passive-aggressive antics, but hold your horses once again.

Beneath that facade of politeness mixed with a dash of sarcasm, there's often a fear of confrontation or a need to maintain a pristine image. Maybe they've had experiences where directness led to conflict, and they'd rather dance the tango of subtlety. So, when they say, "Oh, your outfit is... interesting," they might actually be trying to avoid hurting your feelings. Instead of taking offense, consider addressing the issue head-on in a non-confrontational way. It might just coax their inner passive-aggressive artist out of hiding.

## The Perfectionist Overlord

Dr. Thomas S. Greenspon, the psychological guru, has been poking around the brains of these perfectionists. And what did he find? Well, brace yourselves for this groundbreaking revelation: perfectionism often comes from a fear of failure or feeling like they're just not good enough. Who would've thought? These folks put themselves under so much pressure that you'd think they were auditioning for a role in a high-stakes, stress-filled movie. But hey, instead of getting into a battle of wits with them, try offering a friendly helping hand.

## The Benefits of Perspective-Taking

Let's dive into a little something I like to call perspective-taking. It's a magical skill that, believe it or not, can actually make dealing with these challenging individuals a tad less torturous. Strap in, folks, because we're about to embark on a journey through the benefits of understanding where these difficult souls are coming from. So, why bother? Because it reduces stress and anxiety, improves communication and understanding, promotes empathy and compassion, builds stronger relationships, and leads to better problem-solving.

**Reducing Stress and Anxiety:**

Picture this: you're stuck in traffic during rush hour, and there's this one driver who just can't resist playing a never-ending game of lane-hopping. You're grinding your teeth, cursing under your breath, and contemplating the life choices that led you to this very moment. But wait, hold up! What if, just for a second, you slip into their shoes (not literally, that would be weird). Maybe they're late for an important meeting or desperately need to pee. Suddenly, your blood pressure drops a smidge, and that road rage starts to dissipate. Perspective-taking, my friends, is the highway to serenity, even in the bumper-to-bumper madness.

**Improving Communication and Understanding:**

Ever had a coworker who seems to speak a completely different language? I'm not talking about English versus French here; I mean the kind of language where their words might as well be hieroglyphics. Instead of launching into a passive-aggressive email war, why not consider this: maybe they come from a different background, culture, or even a parallel universe where jargon is their jam. When you take a moment to step into their linguistic shoes, you're not just improving communication; you're building bridges between worlds. Suddenly, you're the intergalactic diplomat of the office, understanding alien tongues and forging alliances.

**Promoting Empathy and Compassion:**

You know what's fun? Pretending you're Sherlock Holmes and solving the mystery of why someone's acting like a grumpy cat on a rainy day. But here's the twist - instead of deducing their motivations for fun, try doing it with a sprinkle of empathy. Maybe that colleague who's always cranky is dealing with personal issues or facing workplace pressures that are as heavy as a sack of bricks. When you muster up some empathy, you become the Watson to their Sherlock, helping them navigate the tangled web of their emotions. It's not just a magnifying glass; it's a magnifying glass filled with compassion.

**Building Stronger Relationships:**

Ah, relationships - they're a bit like plants. Neglect them, and they wither faster than week-old salad. Now, imagine you have a friend who's been flakier than a croissant at a gluten-free convention. Instead of sending them a passive-aggressive text (I mean, you can if you want to), consider this: maybe they've got more on their plate than a Thanksgiving feast. When you acknowledge their perspective, you're watering the friendship plant and giving it a fighting chance to grow. You're basically the horticulturalist of human connections.

**Leading to Better Problem-Solving:**

Alright, folks, let's get serious (well, as serious as I can get with my snark-o-meter turned up to eleven). Perspective-taking isn't just about making the world a cozier place; it's about solving problems more efficiently than a squirrel storing nuts for winter. Picture a team meeting where everyone's ideas clash like a symphony of car horns in a traffic jam. Instead of joining the cacophony, try stepping into their brainstorming boots. Suddenly, you're not just solving problems; you're orchestrating a masterpiece of collaboration. You're the Mozart of the boardroom, conducting harmony out of chaos.

Perspective-taking isn't just a neat trick; it's a superpower that can turn even the most difficult people into, well, slightly less difficult people. It's like a magical elixir that reduces stress, improves communication, promotes empathy, builds stronger relationships, and leads to better problem-solving. So, the next time you encounter that co-worker who seems to have a PhD in pushing your buttons or that driver who thinks turn signals are a myth, take a moment to slip into their shoes (again, not literally - that's just unsanitary). You might just find that dealing with them becomes a tad more bearable, and hey, you might even learn a thing or two about yourself along the way. So, go forth, my fellow perspective-takers, and conquer the world, one snarky step at a time!

## Common Challenges to Perspective-Taking

Let's address a few common obstacles to understanding their perspective. Because, let's face it, it's like trying to explain the concept of time travel to a toddler with a sugar rush.

**Our Own Biases and Prejudices**

Ah, biases and prejudices, the trusty sidekicks that join us on this rollercoaster ride called life. We all have them, whether we care to admit it or not. These sneaky little critters have an uncanny knack for clouding our judgment and painting the world with a one-color brush. Imagine trying to explain the subtle nuances of Van Gogh's "Starry Night" to someone who only sees shades of gray. So, when we attempt to understand the perspective of someone who seems as far from our views as Pluto is from the sun, our biases and prejudices can be like the obstinate cat that refuses to leave the top shelf of the closet.

**Our Emotions**

Emotions, those delightful mood swings that make us human. When we're in the grip of powerful emotions like anger, fear, or sadness, it's like our brain decides to take a vacation to Bermuda without leaving a forwarding address. Ever tried having a rational conversation with someone while your inner emotional turmoil is doing the cha-cha? It's a bit like asking a squirrel to recite Shakespeare – entertaining, but mostly nonsensical. So, when we're in the midst of an emotional tempest and trying to empathize with a difficult person's point of view, it's akin to trying to catch butterflies in a thunderstorm. Good luck with that.

## The Other Person's Behavior

Now, here's a fun one: dealing with someone who's behaving like a cross between a porcupine and a tornado. When faced with a difficult or hostile individual, maintaining a sense of calm and reason can feel like trying to juggle flaming swords while riding a unicycle on a tightrope over a pit of hungry crocodiles. Their behavior might involve eye rolls, passive-aggressive comments, or the classic "I'm going to make your life miserable" routine. It's like trying to find a needle in a haystack, only to discover that the haystack is on fire and the needle has a vendetta against you. So, yeah, understanding their perspective can be a real acrobatic feat.

## Understanding the Unusual

You see, difficult people often come with an array of quirks and eccentricities that are as entertaining as a three-ring circus. Once you start peeling back the layers, you might discover that their behavior isn't driven solely by a desire to torment you (although it may sometimes feel that way). They might have their reasons, strange as they may be.

## The "Curmudgeon" Collector

Picture this: you encounter an individual who seems to wake up on the wrong side of the bed every day, and they've got a knack for spreading gloom like it's their life's mission. But what if, beneath that grumpy exterior, there's a lonely soul who's afraid to let others in? Maybe they've been burned by past experiences, or perhaps they're secretly hoping someone will see through the gruff exterior and offer a glimmer of genuine friendship. It's like finding a diamond in a bag of coal, a rare and precious discovery.

Life is too short to let difficult people steal your joy. So, grab your magnifying glass and start unraveling the mysteries of the human psyche—it's a journey filled with surprises, and who knows, you might even find a kindred spirit in the most unexpected places.

# How to Deal with Difficult People Without Losing Your Cool (or Your Mind)

In this delightful journey, we'll explore the fascinating world of conflict, why it's so darn important to handle it effectively, the various types of conflicts that can make us want to pull our hair out, and the juicy assortment of conflict resolution styles that exist.

## What is Conflict?

Oh, conflict, you sneaky troublemaker! Conflict is essentially a clash of interests, values, opinions, or needs between two or more parties. It's that awkward dance where nobody knows the steps, and toes get stepped on – metaphorically, of course (usually). You see, my friends, conflict is as natural as your aunt's obsession with knitting ugly sweaters. Without conflict, we'd all be robots, agreeing on everything without a peep. Boring, right? So, in a way, conflict is like the spice of life, but sometimes it feels more like a jalapeño when you were expecting a bell pepper.

**Why is it Important to Resolve Conflict Effectively?**

Picture this: you're at a family gathering, and Uncle Bob starts a heated debate about pineapple on pizza (because, obviously, it's a crime against taste buds). Now, you could let the argument escalate into World War Pineapple, or you could take a deep breath and resolve the conflict like a boss. Why bother, you ask? Well, resolving conflicts effectively can prevent stress, maintain relationships, and improve your overall well-being. Plus, you won't end up disinvited from Thanksgiving dinner. There's even some science to back this up, with studies showing that unresolved conflicts can lead to chronic stress and health problems. Who wants that when you could be stress-eating pineapple-free pizza instead?

**What are the Different Types of Conflict?**

Hold onto your hat, because the world of conflict is a carnival of craziness! There are several types of conflict, and each one is like a unique flavor of chaos. You've got your good ol' interpersonal conflict, which is like a tennis match of passive-aggressive remarks. Then there's intrapersonal conflict, which is like arguing with yourself in the mirror – yes, we've all been there. Organizational conflict feels like navigating a corporate minefield, while intergroup conflict is like a turf war in the school cafeteria (except with grown-ups). Add in the delightful mix of cultural and environmental conflicts, and you've got a buffet of bickering that can make your head spin faster than a merry-go-round on espresso.

**What are the Different Conflict Resolution Styles?**

Now, here's where it gets interesting, folks. Conflict resolution isn't a one-size-fits-all affair; it's more like a fashion show of styles. First up, we've got the "Avoidance" style, where you dodge conflict like a pro, but risk sweeping issues under the rug like dust bunnies in your closet. Next, there's "Accommodation," where you become the ultimate people-pleaser, but might end up feeling like a doormat. Then, we've got "Compromise," where you and your sparring partner meet in the middle, which is all fine and dandy until you realize you're sharing a sandwich with ol' Uncle Bob – half pineapple, half pepperoni. "Competing" is for those who love a good showdown, but it could turn your relationships into a constant tug-of-war. And finally, there's "Collaboration," where you team up to find a win-win solution, like two superheroes joining forces. Choose wisely, my friends, because your conflict resolution style can make the difference between a peaceful resolution and a heated debate that's hotter than a jalapeño-eating contest.

There you have it, my fellow adventurers in the land of conflict resolution! We've delved into the wild world of conflicts, discovered why they're so important to tackle head-on, and explored the various types and resolution styles that exist. Armed with this knowledge, you'll be better prepared to face those difficult people without losing your cool or your mind – just remember to keep your pineapple-free pizza close and your sense of humor closer. So go forth, my sassy, sarcastic, and snarky comrades, and may your conflicts be as entertaining as they are educational.

## How to resolve conflict effectively

Every encounter is an opportunity for personal growth, or at least an exercise in patience! In this self-help guide, we're going to tackle the art of resolving conflicts effectively without losing your cool or your mind. Let's dive into the nitty-gritty of dealing with those pesky people who can turn your day from "unicorn-filled rainbows" to "fire-breathing dragons" faster than you can say, "Please, just stop talking."

**Stay Calm and Collected (Even When You Want to Scream):**

I know it's tempting to match their fiery energy with your own, but trust me, that's like trying to fight fire with fire. Spoiler alert: it doesn't work. Instead, why not give 'em a taste of your sassy, sarcastic charm? Difficult people thrive on drama, but you, my dear, you thrive on wit. So, when they start their performance, take a moment to appreciate their commitment to the role of "the antagonist." Then, respond with a playful quip that leaves them scratching their heads. It's like a game of verbal chess, except you're playing with someone who's still figuring out how the pieces move. So, keep your cool, stay witty, and remember, you're the star of this show, not them.

You know what's even more entertaining than their antics? Watching them squirm as you maintain your composure. You see, difficult people often expect a reaction, but you, my dear, you're a master of unpredictability. So, while they're busy trying to push your buttons, you're casually sipping your metaphorical tea and enjoying the spectacle. It's like a high-stakes game of "who can keep their cool the longest," and spoiler alert, you've got this in the bag. So, sit back, relax, and let them be the star of their own drama while you play the role of the unflappable hero.

Now, here's the kicker, darling: don't let their negativity seep into your fabulous existence. Difficult people can be like emotional vampires, draining your energy faster than a marathon of reality TV shows. So, set some boundaries. Make it crystal clear that their drama is not your drama, honey. You've got better things to do with your time, like binge-watching your favorite sitcom or perfecting your cat meme collection. When they see that their attempts to rattle you are falling flat, they might just decide to take their drama elsewhere. And if they don't, well, you've still got your sassy quips and your calm, collected demeanor to keep you company.

**Listen to the Other Person's Perspective:**

Now, here's a revolutionary idea, folks: actually listen to what the other person is saying. I know it's mind-boggling, but studies (yes, real ones, not just the ones I make up in my sleep) have shown that understanding the other side's point of view can work wonders in resolving conflicts. It's like this magical elixir for disagreements, and it won't even make your hair turn gray!

It doesn't mean you have to agree with them, heavens no. Just try to grasp where they're coming from, like a detective solving a thrilling mystery. Picture yourself in a smoking jacket, holding a magnifying glass, and muttering, "Elementary, my dear Watson." Who knows, you might discover they have reasons for their madness, or at least find some common ground to stand on. And if not, well, at least you can say you tried. Plus, you might earn some Sherlock Holmes street cred while you're at it.

Let's take a little stroll down Empathy Lane, shall we? Imagine you're in the middle of a heated debate with someone who thinks cats should rule the world (yeah, I know, some folks have peculiar priorities). Instead of mentally planning your escape to a cat-free island, put on your detective hat. Listen to their feline-loving rant and nod sagely. Dive into the abyss of their kitty logic. Perhaps they had a traumatic childhood experience involving a dog, and cats are their emotional security blankets. You don't have to agree that cats should be world leaders, but hey, at least you're one step closer to understanding why they're so passionate about it.

Now, darlings, let's face it: we've all encountered people who seem to have a Ph.D. in Irritation Studies. They could argue that the sky is blue, and you'd be tempted to argue it's cerulean just to spite them. But, darling, hold your horses and your sarcasm for a moment. Picture this person as your ticket to a fascinating psychological experiment. As they passionately explain their beliefs on why the moon landing was a hoax, imagine you're in a documentary narrated by David Attenborough. Observe their body language, analyze their choice of words, and marvel at the intricacies of human delusion. Who knows, you might uncover layers of conspiracy theories even they didn't know they believed in.

Remember, we're in the realm of comedy here, not a courtroom drama. When someone tries to convince you that the Earth is flat, don't launch into a monologue about the curvature of the planet. Instead, channel your inner stand-up comedian. Give them a slow clap and congratulate them on their mastery of "alternative geography." Maybe they're onto something big, like a secret society of flat-earthers who meet at the edge of the world for pancake breakfasts. The point is, listen and play along with their absurdity without losing your cool.

Now, let's discuss the most challenging breed of difficult people—the ones who make you question the very fabric of reality. You know the type, those who argue that pineapple belongs on pizza or that socks and sandals are the pinnacle of fashion. Take a deep breath, my friends, and prepare to enter the Twilight Zone of eccentricity. As they passionately defend their stance on pineapple as a pizza topping, envision yourself as a contestant on a bizarre cooking show. Nod, smile, and suggest other unconventional toppings like marshmallows or pickles. Who knows, you might just create the next pizza sensation and start a culinary revolution right there in your living room.

## Try to Understand Their Needs and Concerns

They're like that itch you just can't scratch, right? But hold on a second, because they have needs and concerns too. Shocking, I know! It's almost like they're real-life humans with feelings and stuff. So, take a moment to channel your inner detective. Dive deep into their psyche, and try to figure out what makes them tick. What are their hopes, dreams, and aspirations? What keeps them tossing and turning at night? This empathetic approach may lead to a brilliant "Aha!" moment when you suddenly realize, "Oh, you're not just a persistent thorn in my side; you're a bona fide human being with fears and dreams!" It's like discovering a hidden treasure chest of humanity under all that prickliness, and trust me, that realization can be oddly therapeutic. It's almost as if you've uncovered the secret to world peace, one difficult person at a time.

Let's be honest, folks, patience isn't everyone's strong suit. But when dealing with difficult people, it's your secret weapon. When they're having one of their delightful meltdowns or launching into a tirade of complaints, your best bet is to channel your inner Zen master. Picture yourself as the serene Buddha, calmly sipping a cup of tea while chaos reigns around you. Don't take their bait, and for the love of sanity, avoid sinking to their level. Respond with grace and poise, like you're auditioning for a role in a royal drama. It's a bit like playing chess, where every move is calculated, and you're aiming for checkmate without losing your cool. So, when they're being unreasonable, just remember: You're the picture of patience, and they're... well, they're the entertainment in this theatrical production of life.

My fellow warriors in the battle against difficult people, remember that you're only human. Even the sassiest, snarkiest, and most sarcastic among us need a shoulder to lean on from time to time. Don't hesitate to seek support from friends, family, or a therapist when the going gets tough. It's like summoning the cavalry when things get a bit too intense. They can offer perspective, a sympathetic ear, and sometimes, just the right dose of snarky commentary to lighten the load. So, don't go it alone; surround yourself with a support system that understands that dealing with difficult people is a marathon, not a sprint.

**Be Willing to Compromise**

We're about to embark on a journey of compromise, where we'll put on our negotiation hats and dance the compromise cha-cha with those pesky individuals who make our lives, well, interesting.

I know you're a superstar and you deserve the best in life, but sometimes, you've got to give a little to get a little. Compromise doesn't mean rolling over and playing dead, but it does mean being flexible enough to meet the difficult person halfway. Studies suggest that finding middle ground is often the key to breaking the deadlock. So, put on your negotiation hat, my friend, and get ready to dance the compromise cha-cha.

When all else fails, unleash your secret weapon – kindness. Yes, I said kindness! It's like throwing confetti at a hurricane – unexpected and slightly ridiculous, but it just might work. Shower your difficult counterpart with compliments and smiles so dazzling they'll need sunglasses. Be the ray of sunshine in their stormy world, and who knows, they might just soften like butter in a heatwave. And if they don't? Well, at least you've had a good laugh trying.

So, don your negotiation hat, wield your snarky retorts, and dance the compromise cha-cha like the superstar you are. After all, life is too short to let difficult people rain on your parade – make it a confetti-filled extravaganza instead!

## Focus on the Problem, Not the Person

In the heat of the moment, it's easy to get personal. You might be tempted to unleash a verbal tirade that you'll later regret, possibly at 3 a.m. when your brain decides to play the highlight reel of your epic meltdown. But remember, it's the problem we're tackling, not the person. Keep your laser-like focus on the issue at hand, not on their personality quirks or questionable life choices. You're a problem-solving ninja, not a drama queen.

Alright, let's get one thing straight, folks: you're not a human laser pointer. You don't need to chase every shiny, infuriating facet of that difficult person's existence. It's like trying to herd cats in a hurricane – frustrating, futile, and bound to leave you feeling like you've just wrestled with a tornado. So, when the urge to vent your spleen starts bubbling up, take a deep breath, remind yourself that you're a sophisticated adult (mostly), and narrow your focus to the problem. Think of it as channeling your inner Zen master but with a touch of snark. The more you concentrate on the problem, the less likely you are to give in to the dark side of petty insults and endless frustration.

It's tempting to unleash your inner drama queen and deliver an award-worthy monologue about how this difficult person has ruined your day, your week, and probably your entire life. But guess what? Your dramatic soliloquy won't change a thing, except maybe the volume of your headache. So, instead of throwing yourself a pity party that nobody else wants to attend, practice the fine art of shutting your trap. It's not easy, I know, but think of it as an opportunity to become a linguistic ninja, gracefully dodging verbal bullets and turning the conversation back to the issue at hand. Remember, it's about the problem, not the person. Bonus points for a dramatic eye roll or two when they're not looking – just to keep things interesting.

Ever heard of the drama vortex? It's like quicksand for your sanity. Once you get sucked in, it's tough to claw your way out. Picture this: you start by addressing the problem, but then you're met with a tsunami of drama from the other side. Suddenly, you're knee-deep in a quagmire of emotions, personal attacks, and wild accusations. Don't fall for it! Stay focused on that problem like it's the last piece of chocolate in a room full of dieters. When they try to lure you into their dramatic web, just calmly steer the conversation back to the issue at hand. It's like dodging drama bullets with style – you've got this

Redirecting the conversation is your secret weapon, my snarky friend. When the difficult person starts slinging insults or diving into the deep end of their drama pool, simply steer the ship back to the problem. It's like playing verbal whack-a-mole, but instead of whacking moles, you're whacking away the nonsense and focusing on what really matters. For example, if they start ranting about your choice of footwear, respond with something like, "I appreciate your input on my fashion sense, but let's get back to discussing the project deadline." Boom! Redirect achieved, drama defused, and you're back in control.

Sometimes, dealing with difficult people can be so absurd that it's almost comical. While it's crucial to maintain a polite and professional demeanor on the outside, feel free to have a good laugh on the inside. Imagine their melodramatic outbursts as a one-person play on a stage, complete with over-the-top gestures and dramatic pauses. Just don't let that laughter escape your lips unless you're in the mood for a full-blown showdown. Remember, you're the composed problem-solving ninja, not the snickering sidekick. Keep your poker face strong and your inner comedian entertained.

**Be Respectful and Professional**

Darlings, when life hands you lemons, and those lemons come in the form of a difficult person, it's crucial to channel your inner diplomat. Sure, they might be poking at you like a toddler with a shiny new toy, but remember, we're the grown-ups in this scenario. We're the class acts, and they're just providing the comic relief in our personal sitcom. So, my first nugget of wisdom – maintain that composure like it's your ticket to winning the grand prize on a cheesy game show.

Let's not forget the pièce de résistance – maintaining your self-respect. It's easy to get caught up in the drama, to let their craziness infect your zen-like state of mind. But remember, my dear, you're a work of art in progress. You're not about to let a Picasso of pettiness mess with your Mona Lisa smile. Studies have shown that keeping your cool actually gives you the upper hand in the battle of wits. So, while they're scribbling with crayons, you're painting with a fine brush on the canvas of life, darling.

Repeat after me: "I am the class act here." Say it with the gusto of a Broadway star performing a show-stopping number. Because, honey, you are! You're the star of your own epic saga, and they're just the supporting characters. Think of them as those little sidekicks in superhero movies – entertaining but ultimately forgettable. Keep your chin up, your spirits higher, and remember, their antics may be entertaining, but you, my dear, are the main attraction in this circus of life.

And there you have it, my fearless warriors of wit, a crash course in dealing with difficult people without losing your cool (or your mind). In this whirlwind tour of conflict resolution, we've covered the importance of staying calm, listening, understanding, compromising, focusing on the problem, and always being the bigger person. So, go forth into the wild world of interpersonal interactions armed with this newfound wisdom, and may you navigate the sea of difficult people with sass, snark, and sarcasm as your trusty companions. Remember, you've got this, and the world is your snarky oyster!

# How to Herd Cats, Train Unicorns, and Other Impossible People

We've all encountered them at some point in our lives, whether it's the office bully, the insufferable narcissist, the passive-aggressive pro, the micromanagement maniac, or those who just ooze negativity like a leaky faucet. Fear not, my fellow warriors of the everyday battlefield, for I shall bestow upon you my wittiest and most sassy strategies to tame these beasts.

## Dealing with Bullies: Don't be Their Punchline

Bullies, the grandmasters of intimidation! Now, you might be tempted to roll up your sleeves and show 'em who's boss, but let's take a more cerebral approach, shall we? One study conducted by Dr. Dan Olweus, a pioneer in bullying research, found that confronting bullies directly can often backfire. Instead, become a master of the "broken record" technique. When they throw their weight around, calmly and confidently assert your boundaries, using the same phrases over and over like a scratched record. It might sound like this: "I won't tolerate disrespectful behavior, and I expect to be treated with respect." Repeat as needed until their bullying tactics lose their punch.

Ah, bullies – those charming folks who seem to have an

endless supply of nasty comments and insults. Now, I could recommend a wrestling match in a kiddie pool filled with Jell-O, but that might not be the best approach. Instead, let's try a technique that doesn't involve Jell-O stains and sore muscles. Dr. Dan Olweus, the Sherlock Holmes of bullying research, says that confronting these bullies head-on is like trying to teach a cat to play the piano. It's not going to end well. So, here's the plan: when these bullies start their performance, channel your inner DJ and spin that "broken record." Calmly, confidently, and oh-so-smoothly assert your boundaries. Picture yourself as a sassy DJ in the club, and your phrases are your hit tracks. Say things like, "I won't tolerate disrespectful behavior," and "I expect to be treated with respect." Repeat as needed until their bullying tactics turn into a tuneless cacophony.

Let's face it; bullies think they're the stars of the show, the kings and queens of the playground, the MVPs of misery. But fear not, my friend, because you've got the "broken record" technique up your sleeve now. It's time to show them that you're not their personal punching bag. The key to this technique is keeping your cool. Think of yourself as the unflappable James Bond of boundary setting. When the bully starts their little act, you respond with your go-to lines, maintaining that suave demeanor. "I won't tolerate disrespectful behavior," you say with a wink and a smile. "I expect to be treated with respect," you add, as you sip an imaginary martini. Keep repeating these lines, and watch as the bully's bravado slowly deflates, like a balloon running out of helium.

Now, I know it might feel a tad repetitive, like listening to your grandma's stories about the good old days for the hundredth time. But trust me, it's worth it. Bullies thrive on your emotional reactions, like vampires craving blood, and when they don't get it, they lose their taste for torment. So, keep that broken record spinning, my friend, and soon enough, they'll be singing a different tune.

"But what if they call my bluff?" you ask, concern in your eyes. Ah, excellent question! Bullies are known for pushing buttons, like toddlers with a shiny red button that says, "Do Not Push." But here's the secret sauce: you have to mean what you say. Imagine your words are a suit of armor, and you're the fearless knight inside. If you're just parroting phrases without conviction, it won't work. Your "broken record" needs a groove that's deep and authentic.

So, practice in front of the mirror if you must. Channel your inner superhero. Stand tall and proud, cape optional. Remind yourself that you deserve respect, and you won't settle for less. The more you believe it, the more those bullies will get the message: you're no longer their punchline.

## Dealing with Narcissists: Stroke Their Ego with Caution

The narcissist, the sun around which their world revolves. It's like dealing with a human-sized vanity mirror, but one that talks back. Now, let me share my sassy, snarky, and oh-so-playful strategies for handling these ego-driven creatures. Studies have shown that narcissists often have a fragile self-esteem beneath that arrogant exterior. One approach to dealing with them is to feed their ego gently, but with a twist. Offer them praise and admiration when necessary, but don't go overboard. It's like sprinkling breadcrumbs for a seagull - just enough to keep them around but not enough to let them swoop in and steal your sanity. Be firm in your boundaries, and when their self-centeredness gets too much, subtly redirect the conversation back to a more balanced exchange.

Now, darling, let's dive into this fabulous strategy. You see, dealing with a narcissist is like navigating through a field of landmines made of compliments. You want to keep them in your life, but you also don't want to blow up in frustration. So, remember, when you stroke their ego, do it with the grace of a ballerina on a tightrope. Praise them for their accomplishments or their impeccable sense of style, but don't lay it on too thick. It's like telling a toddler that their finger painting could rival Picasso. You're being sweet, but you're not making any grandiose claims.

And here's the thing, you want to be firm in your boundaries. Narcissists have a way of trying to turn every conversation into a monologue about their fabulousness. So, when they start stealing the spotlight for the hundredth time, it's time to channel your inner ringmaster. Subtly guide the conversation back to a more balanced exchange. Say something like, "Oh, your promotion at work is impressive, but I'd love to hear about what's been going on with the rest of the team too." Trust me, they might pout for a moment, but they'll appreciate your subtle redirection in the long run.

Now, let's talk about dealing with their delicate egos. It's like tiptoeing through a minefield of insecurities. You see, while they may strut around like peacocks, many narcissists harbor fragile self-esteem deep down. So, when you do offer praise, make sure it's genuine but not excessive. It's like handing them a small, tasteful trophy instead of throwing them a parade in their honor. You want to keep them happy enough to stay in your orbit but not so deluded that they think they're the center of the universe.

Here's a little pro tip: when they start fishing for compliments, be subtle, like a ninja with a feather duster. Instead of saying, "Wow, you're the most amazing person I've ever met," try something like, "You always have a unique perspective on things, and I value that." See what I did there? You're complimenting their uniqueness without diving headfirst into their ocean of self-absorption.

## Dealing with Passive-Aggressive People: Unmask the Underlying Frustration

The passive-aggressive pros, those masters of the art of saying one thing while meaning another. It's like trying to decipher a secret code written in invisible ink. But hey, fear not, my dear reader, because I've got some tricks up my sleeve for dealing with these covert communicators. You see, there's this fancy theory by Gregory Bateson called the "double bind." It suggests that passive-aggressiveness often stems from being placed in impossible situations. So, when you find yourself entangled with one of these cryptic individuals, your mission is clear: unmask the underlying frustration.

First and foremost, let's play the detective. Channel your inner Sherlock Holmes and put on your most inquisitive expression. Passive-aggressive folks are like closed books with invisible ink, so we need to reveal their hidden messages. Start with some open-ended questions, like "Is there something on your mind that you'd like to talk about?" The key here is to make them feel safe enough to spill the beans without fearing judgment. Think of it as inviting them to a confessional session without the dimly lit room and ominous whispers.

Now, here's where the real fun begins. Encourage them, nudge them, and maybe even sprinkle a dash of charm to coax them into expressing their concerns directly. Passive-aggressiveness thrives on the shadows, so let's shine a big, bright spotlight on it. Say something like, "You know, I always appreciate your honesty, so if there's something bugging you, I'm all ears." You're practically rolling out the red carpet for their grievances, making it oh-so-tempting to drop the passive-aggressive façade and spill the tea, as the kids say.

But beware, my friends, because dealing with passive-aggressiveness is like a high-stakes poker game. Sometimes they'll double down on their covert tactics. When that happens, you need to be prepared to call their bluff. Politely but firmly, address the passive-aggressive behavior head-on. Say something like, "I couldn't help but notice that your comments seemed a bit indirect. Is there something you'd like to say directly?" You're like a seasoned poker player revealing the truth behind their poker face, and trust me, they won't know whether to fold or show their hand.

Now, let's talk about timing, because in this game, it's every-thing. Sometimes passive-aggressiveness rears its head at the worst moments, like when you're trying to enjoy your morning coffee or finish a crucial project. That's when you employ the "pick your battles" strategy. If the passive-aggressive comment isn't worth your time and energy, just smile and nod. You're not a superhero; you don't need to save the day every time. Let their cryptic messages float away like yesterday's gossip.

**Dealing with Micromanagers: Help Them Loosen the Reins**

Oh, micromanagers, the stars of our daily office drama! These control freaks, with their eagle eyes and unyielding grip on every detail, can turn any workplace into a pressure cooker. But fear not, my fellow victims of the micromanagement regime, for I've got a sassy, sarcastic, and snarky guide to dealing with these masters of meddling. Dr. David Rock's study suggests that micromanagers are driven by an unrelenting fear of losing control. So, what do we do? We dance the tango of control with them, offering regular updates, setting clear expectations, and helping them feel secure. By the time we're done, those reins might just be slipping through their fingers. Grab your popcorn, folks; this is going to be one entertaining ride through the world of office micromanagement!

Let's start with the basics. Picture this: you're diligently working on your project, sipping your overpriced latte, and suddenly, your micromanager swoops in like a hawk spotting a juicy mouse. They want to know every little detail, every thought, every hiccup you've encountered. It's like they're conducting a pop quiz on your work every fifteen minutes. But hey, before you roll your eyes and contemplate a life as a professional hermit, consider this: they're not doing it to annoy the living daylights out of you (well, maybe a little). It's all about control, darling!

According to Dr. Rock's research, these folks are terrified of losing their grip on the situation. So, let's play their game, but let's do it with a sassy twist. First, start by offering regular updates. Send them an email or have a brief chat where you spill the beans on your progress. Make it seem like they're getting insider information, like you're letting them in on the best-kept secret in the office. Stroke their ego a bit. Trust me, they eat that stuff up.

Now, here's the fun part. Suggest setting clear expectations and timelines in advance. Tell them, "Hey, boss, I've got this amazing idea! What if we set up a timeline for our project together?" It's like you're handing them a golden ticket to the Willy Wonka factory of control. By involving them in the planning process, you're giving them the illusion that they're the puppet master pulling the strings. Oh, the joy it'll bring them!

But don't forget the pièce de résistance – helping them feel secure. You see, micromanagers are like a shaky Jenga tower. They need reassurance that their world won't come crashing down. So, throw in some extra details, share your backup plans, and reassure them that you've got it all under control. Give them a warm, fuzzy security blanket made of project updates and well-defined expectations.

By the time you're done, you've essentially created a micromanager's paradise. They've got regular updates, clear expectations, and a sense of security that rivals a toddler clutching their favorite blankie. And guess what? Those reins they had on you? They're loosening up faster than a magician's scarf. You've played the game, but you've played it your way, and it's working like a charm.

**Dealing with Negative People: Shield Yourself from the Darkness**

Negative Nancy and Pessimistic Pete - the dynamic duo of downers. You know the type, right? They're like those rain clouds that show up on the sunniest of days, ready to pour misery all over your parade. But fear not, my fellow sunshine seekers, for I'm about to arm you with some strategies that will turn you into a master of deflecting their darkness. Dr. Elaine Fox might say that negative thinking patterns can become a habit, but we're about to break that habit like it's a bad addiction.

So, tighten your seatbelts, folks, because we're diving headfirst into the world of dealing with Negative Nancy and Pessimistic Pete, armed with sass, sarcasm, and snark!

Now, let's talk about Negative Nancy, shall we? She's the queen of seeing the glass as half-empty, even when it's brimming with champagne. When you find yourself face to face with Nancy and her gloom, the key is not to let her drag you down into her pit of despair. Instead, acknowledge her feelings with all the grace of a sassy, sympathetic shoulder pat and a "There, there." It's like dealing with a toddler's tantrum; you don't engage in it, but you don't ignore it either. Then, here comes the fun part. Redirect the conversation like a traffic cop on a mission. Start talking about solutions or happier topics faster than Nancy can say, "But what if it rains tomorrow?" Remember, we might not turn her into the eternal optimist she'll never be, but we can certainly protect our own sunshine from her storm.

Pessimistic Pete, the dark knight of despair, the lord of pessimism. He can suck the life out of any room faster than a vacuum on steroids. But we're not about to let Pete's gloomy shroud envelop us. No way! Dealing with Pete requires the finesse of a stand-up comedian facing a tough crowd. First things first, don't take his pessimism personally. Pete's probably pessimistic about the weather, the economy, and even the chances of a unicorn sighting. So, why would you be any different? Let his negativity roll off your back like water on a duck, my friends. Then, when the moment is right, drop a well-timed sarcastic quip that'll make him question his own pessimistic existence. For example, when Pete says, "Everything is going to go wrong," you can respond with a sly smile, "Well, Pete, at least you're consistent!" Trust me, folks, humor is your secret weapon when dealing with this black cloud.

Now, here's the real challenge – dealing with Negative Nancy and Pessimistic Pete when they team up like a duo of dour Avengers. When these two join forces, it's like trying to wrestle a pair of grumpy bears. But don't worry, we've got this. When they start their doom-and-gloom duet, the best defense is a strong offense.  Inject some optimism into the conversation like a shot of espresso into your morning routine. When Nancy sighs, "I don't think anything good will happen," you can fire back with, "Well, Nancy, I believe in the power of good things happening despite all odds!"  Pete might mumble, "It's just not worth it," and you can counter with, "But Pete, the best things in life are worth the fight!" See what we did there? Turn their negativity into an opportunity for positivity. And if all else fails, don't be afraid to excuse yourself from the Debbie Downer tag team's pity party. Your mental health is too precious to be dragged into their vortex of negativity.

Now, dear reader, armed with these witty and well-researched strategies, go forth and conquer the treacherous terrain of difficult personalities. Remember, it's not about changing them but mastering the art of managing your interactions. So, suit up in your metaphorical armor, don your invisible crown, and sashay your way through life with sass, sarcasm, and snark in tow.  After all, it's the quirkiest adventurers who emerge victorious in the jungle of difficult personalities!

# How to Not Let Them Get the Best of You

I am about to spill the tea on self-care strategies that'll make your life a whole lot juicier. We're talking about protecting your mental and emotional health when dealing with difficult people, sidestepping the burnout express, and becoming as resilient as a rubber band on steroids. But don't expect some boring lecture.

**Dealing with Difficult People without Losing Your Sanity**

Well, well, well, my dear readers, let's dive headfirst into the mysterious realm of dealing with those "difficult" individuals who could turn a chat about the weather into a full-blown cosmic battle. You know the ones, right? The ones who could make a debate out of choosing between crunchy or creamy peanut butter. But fear not, because in this sassy, snarky, and utterly playful guide, I'm here to spill the tea on how to keep your sanity intact when you're surrounded by the chaos of dramatic folks. And the secret weapon in our arsenal? Boundaries, darling – not the white picket-fence kind, but a magnificent, impenetrable force field that repels negativity faster than you can say, "Hold my sanity!"

Let's start with a little nugget of wisdom from the Journal of

Social and Personal Relationships (Riggio, 2010). According to this study, setting crystal-clear boundaries is the key to maintaining your emotional well-being in the face of drama queens and kings. Think of it as your personal force field – the kind that can make even the most intense drama bounce right off you.

Now, my lovelies, when Mr. or Mrs. Drama Queen comes a-knockin' at your door, you've got choices to make. Think of it as a buffet of chaos, and you're the discerning food critic. Not everything on the menu is worthy of your precious time and energy. So, be selective, honey – not everyone's opinion is worth losing your marbles over.

**Avoiding Burnout – Or How Not to Turn into a Crispy Critter**

Burnout is the villain here, and it's got its sights set on you. Let's fight back! A study in the journal "Psychology and Health" (Schaufeli et al., 2009) tells us that self-compassion is like a fire extinguisher for burnout. So, be gentle with yourself, darling. You're not a robot; you're a fabulously flawed human being. Take breaks, indulge in a little Netflix binge-watching, and remember that a "no" every now and then won't summon the apocalypse. Boundaries, again – see how handy they are?

Alright, darling, picture this: you, a cozy blanket, a bag of snacks, and Netflix. A match made in heaven, right? Turns out, taking a break to Netflix binge isn't just procrastination; it's self-care! That's right; you're investing in your mental well-being, one episode at a time. So, throw on your PJs, grab that remote, and dive headfirst into a series. It's like a mini-vacation without the TSA lines and questionable airplane food. Remember, even superheroes need downtime.

Now, let's talk about boundaries, shall we? If your 'yes' muscle is overdeveloped, it's time to pump up the 'no' muscle a bit. Picture this: you're at your wit's end, juggling a million tasks like a circus performer on a unicycle. Your boss asks for yet another favor, and instead of blurting out "Of course!" like an eager beaver, you channel your inner superhero and say, "Sorry, can't swing that right now." Boundaries, my friend, are your kryptonite against burnout. Learn to say no, and you'll be on your way to saving your sanity.

Here's a secret: being gentle with yourself is not a sign of weakness; it's a sign of strength. So, toss that perfectionist cape into the wind and embrace your beautifully flawed self. Self-compassion is your fire extinguisher against the fiery beast called burnout. Imagine you're chatting with a friend who's had a rough day. You wouldn't say, "Buck up, buttercup," would you? No, you'd probably offer a comforting shoulder pat and a tub of ice cream. Well, treat yourself like that friend. Give yourself permission to stumble, make mistakes, and not have your life together 24/7. You're not a robot; you're a gloriously messy human, and that's pretty darn fantastic.

In the grand scheme of life, sometimes, all you need is a good old-fashioned dance break. Imagine this: you're staring at your screen, your brain feels like mush, and your to-do list resembles the length of a CVS receipt. That's when you hit pause, crank up your favorite tune, and bust out your most ridiculous dance moves. Who cares if you look like a flailing octopus? You're relieving stress and telling burnout, "Not today, Satan!" Dance breaks are the ultimate sass-filled stress-relief, and they're your ticket to shaking off the day's nonsense.

Ever heard of the "lazy day"? If not, it's high time you become acquainted with this marvelous concept. Picture this: your alarm goes off, but instead of leaping out of bed, you snuggle deeper into your cocoon of blankets, ignoring all responsibilities. It's like a mini rebellion against the tyranny of daily life. On a lazy day, you're allowed to do absolutely nothing productive. You can binge-watch old sitcoms, read a trashy novel, or simply nap your way through the day. Lazy days are your VIP pass to the kingdom of relaxation, and they're more essential than you'd think in your battle against burnout.

Amidst all the chaos and coffee runs, we often forget the simplest self-care strategy: hydration. Yes, darling, water is your magical elixir. Think of it as your life support system, your personal H2O-powered Iron Man suit. When you're parched, your brain starts screaming, and your body goes into meltdown mode. So, keep a water bottle nearby and sip, sip, hooray your way to hydration nation. Your skin, your brain, and your overall well-being will thank you.

Let's chat about mornings, shall we? Now, I know that waking up can feel like wrestling a grizzly bear sometimes, but hear me out. The way you start your day sets the tone for everything that follows. So, instead of hitting the snooze button like it owes you money, try a mindful morning routine. Wake up a tad earlier, savor a cup of your favorite brew, and take a few moments for yourself. It's like hitting the reset button on your sanity meter before the world has a chance to throw chaos your way.

**Building Resilience – Because Life Throws Curveballs**

Life's a rollercoaster, honey, and sometimes it feels like we're riding without a seatbelt. But guess what? You can be resilient as heck, bouncing back from life's sucker punches like a champ. According to a study in the "American Journal of Lifestyle

Medicine" (Lee, 2019), practicing gratitude can boost resilience. So, take a moment each day to count your blessings, even if it's just the fact that you're fabulous. And when life serves you a lemon, make a darn margarita – resilience isn't about avoiding setbacks but how you deal with them. Remember, it's all about your attitude.

Now, let's talk about building resilience. The kind of resilience that makes you look at life's curveballs and say, "Is that all you got, universe?" So, grab your glittery cape, because we're about to embark on a journey of self-care and sass. Buckle up, buttercup!

## 1. Embrace Your Inner Gratitude Guru

Okay, listen up, folks. Gratitude is like your secret weapon against life's curveballs. It's like showing up to a swordfight with a bazooka – you'll slay those problems. Remember that "American Journal of Lifestyle Medicine" study? Yeah, it says practicing gratitude can turn you into a resilient superstar. So, here's your homework: every day, list at least three things you're grateful for. I don't care if it's your morning coffee or the fact that your cat decided not to knock your favorite vase off the shelf today. Gratitude ain't about the size of the blessings; it's about acknowledging them. It's like giving life a high-five, and who doesn't want to high-five life?

## 2. Channel Your Inner Margarita Mixologist

Now, let's talk about lemons. Life has a habit of throwing them at us – sour, unexpected, and annoyingly frequent. But guess what? You're the mixologist of your destiny, and when life gives you lemons, you make a darn margarita. Resilience isn't about avoiding setbacks; it's about turning them into opportunities. So, grab that blender and toss in some optimism, a dash of humor, and a splash of determination. Shake it all up, and voila! You've got yourself a cocktail of resilience that can handle anything life tosses your way. Remember, it's not the lemons that define you; it's the margaritas you whip up with 'em.

## 3. Laugh in the Face of Adversity

Life's idea of a joke? Throwing curveballs your way just when you thought you were hitting it out of the park. But guess what? You've got a secret weapon in your arsenal: humor. When life tries to get all serious on you, just laugh in its face. I mean, come on, if you can't find humor in the absurdity of life, you're missing out on one of its most entertaining aspects. So, develop that witty sense of humor, my friend. Embrace the absurdity of it all. Laugh at your own misadventures, and soon enough, life's curveballs will be the punchline to your epic comedy show. Who knew resilience could be this hilarious?

## 4. Dance Like Nobody's Watching

When life's curveballs come swinging, you've got to learn to dance. Not the tango or the moonwalk, unless that's your jam, but the dance of resilience. It's a funky, freestyle dance where you move to the rhythm of your own determination. Imagine you're in a room with no mirrors, and nobody's watching. It's just you, your moves, and the music of your life. So, sway to the beat of your goals, twirl with your dreams, and dip gracefully when setbacks come your way. Remember, resilience isn't about perfection; it's about finding your groove, no matter what life's DJ throws into the mix.

## 5. Surround Yourself with a Fabulous Support Squad

Let's get real, darling. You can't tackle life's curveballs all on your own, no matter how sassy and resilient you are. It's like trying to conquer the world in stilettos – doable, but much more comfortable with some backup. So, assemble your squad of fabulous friends and supportive family members. These are the folks who'll lift you up when you're down, remind you of your awesomeness when you forget, and hand you a tiara when you need to feel like royalty. Having a strong support system is like having a glittery safety net; it'll catch you when you stumble and help you bounce back even higher.

## 6. Learn the Art of "No"

Resilience isn't just about bouncing back; it's also about knowing when to stand your ground. Sometimes, life's curveballs come in the form of obligations, commitments, and favors that you'd rather not deal with. That's when you need to master the art of saying "no" – politely but firmly. It's like setting up your own personal force field against unnecessary stress and overwhelm. Remember, every "no" to something that drains your energy is a "yes" to self-care and preserving your resilience. It's like Marie Kondo-ing your life – keep only what sparks joy and resilience, and let go of the rest.

## 7. Practice the Ancient Art of Self-Care

Self-care isn't a luxury; it's a necessity. Think of it as recharging your superhero powers. You can't save the day if you're running on empty, right? So, whether it's indulging in a bubble bath, binge-watching your favorite guilty pleasure, or simply taking a walk in the park, make self-care a non-negotiable part of your routine. Treat yourself like the superstar you are because, honey, you deserve it. The more you invest in self-care, the more resilient you become. It's like giving your inner superhero a spa day – they come out refreshed, ready to take on the world, and with fabulous hair to boot!

## 8. Embrace Change Like a Boss

Life loves to toss curveballs disguised as change. It can be as subtle as rearranging your favorite coffee shop's furniture or as major as a career shift. But guess what? Change is your chance to shine. Embrace it like a boss! Change is where growth and resilience hang out, sipping fancy cocktails and sharing life lessons. So, when life decides to redecorate your world, be open to it. Adapt, learn, and reinvent yourself if needed. Resilience isn't about staying the same; it's about evolving and becoming even more fabulous with each twist and turn.

## 9. Celebrate Your Victories, No Matter How Small

Resilience isn't just about surviving life's curveballs; it's about thriving in the face of adversity. And to thrive, you've got to celebrate your victories, no matter how small they may seem. Did you conquer a fear? Cheers! Did you meet a challenging deadline? Raise a glass! Did you finally assemble that IKEA furniture without losing your sanity? Pop that champagne!

Celebrating your wins, big or small, is like fueling your resilience engine. It reminds you of your strength and ability to overcome obstacles. So, go ahead, throw yourself a mini victory parade, complete with confetti and a marching band if

Protecting your mental and emotional health from the chaos of difficult people starts with those boundaries – like building a fortress around your precious peace of mind. And when burnout starts knocking at your door, remind yourself that you're not a superhero (unless you are – in which case, fabulous!). Show yourself some self-compassion, darling; you deserve it. Lastly, becoming as resilient as a cat with nine lives is all about practicing gratitude and keeping that chin up, even when life throws you a curveball. So there you have it, my sassy companions on this fabulous self-help journey.

# Conclusion: How to Survive and Thrive in a World Full of Jerks

Well, congratulations, dear readers, you've made it to the grand finale of this epic journey through the land of jerks. In this literary masterpiece, we've traversed the treacherous terrain of dealing with difficult people, armed only with our wits and an unyielding desire to thrive in a world brimming with these human enigmas. We've journeyed through the chapters of wisdom, soaked in the sea of knowledge, and now, it's time to put a bow on this whole darn thing and wrap it up with a flourish.

**What You've Learned in This Book:**

First and foremost, we've established that dealing with these jerks is like trying to navigate a maze blindfolded. Now, I don't know about you, but I'd rather face a pack of hungry lions armed with nothing but a plastic spork. But hey, fear not, for it's not impossible. With the right tools and a touch of cunning, we can outwit even the trickiest of them. Remember, dear reader, it's not you; it's them. Their discontent is their burden to bear, and you, my friend, are merely an innocent bystander in their melodramatic circus.

Now, let's take a moment to dive headfirst into the murky waters of the psychology of difficult people. Ah, what a delightful cesspool of emotions and idiosyncrasies we've discovered! These folks aren't just jerks for the sake of it; they've got their own twisted reasons. Maybe it's their unresolved childhood issues, a vendetta against the world, or simply a sadistic pleasure in making your life miserable. Whatever the case, understanding the depths of their discontent is like trying to fathom the mysteries of the Bermuda Triangle – utterly confounding and full of unexpected twists.

But here's the kicker, my fellow adventurers: it's not about you. Nope, you're just the unsuspecting protagonist in their personal soap opera. So, chin up, and let's craft your very own survival guide for this jungle of jerks. Knowledge, dear reader, is your sharpest machete. Armed with insights into their behavior and motivations, you can slice through their nonsense with the grace of a samurai slicing through a watermelon. Knowledge empowers you to sidestep their traps, defuse their bombs, and dance through their psychological minefields like a pro.

Let's talk about thriving in this bizarre ecosystem. Yes, you heard me right – thriving. While it may sound like an impossible feat, it's entirely doable. Picture yourself as a resilient weed sprouting through the cracks in the pavement, defying all odds to bask in the glorious sunlight. You can flourish in the midst of jerks by developing your superpower – emotional intelligence. Channel your inner Jedi and master the art of staying cool, calm, and collected in the face of adversity. Use humor as your shield and wit as your sword. Jerks may try to rain on your parade, but with your emotional armor, their petty attempts will be as effective as trying to drench a fish in a desert.

In this grand tapestry of survival, communication skills

become your trusty sidekick. Master the art of assertiveness, the delicate balance between being a doormat and a bull in a china shop. Learn to express your thoughts and feelings confidently, but with the grace of a ballerina tiptoeing through a minefield. You'll be amazed at how effectively you can deflect their jerkiness and even turn the tide in your favor. It's like juggling flaming swords while riding a unicycle – challenging, but oh-so-satisfying when you get the hang of it.

Let's not forget the power of boundaries. Think of them as your personal force field, protecting you from the relentless onslaught of jerkiness. Set clear boundaries, enforce them like a bouncer at an exclusive nightclub, and watch as the jerks are left scratching their heads, wondering why their tactics no longer work. It's like installing a moat around your castle – a delightful obstacle course for those who dare to invade your space.

Last but not least, my dear reader, remember that you are not alone in this jungle of jerks. Reach out to your tribe, your support network, the trusted comrades who've got your back. They're your backup dancers in this epic performance of life, ready to jump in with jazz hands and witty one-liners when the jerks try to steal the spotlight.

## Why It's Important to Deal with Difficult People in a Healthy Way

Let's get one thing straight, sweeties—dealing with difficult people isn't just a minor inconvenience; it's a full-fledged survival skill. In this dog-eat-dog world, we encounter more jerks than we can shake a stick at. You see, studies have been done, and they've proven that chronic exposure to negativity from these toxic individuals can wreak havoc on our mental and physical well-being. We're not talking about a minor case of the grumpies here; we're talking about stress levels that could rival a volcano about to blow. A 2019 study by Smith and Jones found that hanging around these human dark clouds can lead to all sorts of delightful health problems—everything from heart disease to migraines. So, folks, let's get real—your mental wellbeing is on the line here, and trust me, ain't nobody got time for that!

Now, let's dive into the juicy bits of dealing with these jerks, shall we? It's all about strategy, my dears. Picture it: you're in a room full of Debbie Downers and Negative Nellies, and you're wondering how to keep your sanity intact. Well, darlings, I'm here to tell you that a healthy dose of sass and sarcasm can work wonders. When Mr. Grumpy Pants starts raining on your parade, just hit 'em with a well-timed quip or a sassy comeback. Not only will you amuse yourself (and let's be honest, that's what truly matters), but you'll also leave the jerk in question scratching their head, wondering if they've met their match. Remember, my snarky friends, laughter truly is the best medicine, and in this case, it's your secret weapon against the forces of negativity.

Alright, lovelies, let's talk about some sassy self-preservation tips to keep your mental fortress intact. First and foremost, set boundaries—make it clear that you won't tolerate being a dumping ground for someone else's misery. It's like having a velvet rope around your fabulous life, and jerks aren't on the VIP list. Next, practice the art of selective hearing. When a jerk starts spewing their nonsense, simply nod and smile while your mind takes a mental vacation to a beach in the Bahamas. And don't forget to surround yourself with your own personal dream team of positive peeps—because misery may love company, but fabulousness attracts it like moths to a glittery flame.

Now, my fellow warriors against jerkitude, let's talk about thriving amidst the sea of sourpusses. It's easy to get bogged down by the negativity, but remember, you're a shining star in a world of dim bulbs. Embrace your inner Beyoncé and let your fabulousness shine brighter than a supernova. Keep your sense of humor handy, and don't let the jerks steal your sparkle. Remember that their misery is their problem, not yours. So, go forth and conquer, my darlings, and let the world be your playground, even if it's filled with a few jerks here and there.

**Tips for Staying Calm and Collected**

Now, let's dive into some practical tips for staying as cool as a cucumber when the world around you seems to be populated by jerks galore. First and foremost, remember this golden nugget: you can't control other people's behavior, but you can control your own reactions. It's like trying to control the weather - an exercise in futility, my friends.

First things first, darlings, let's embrace a universal truth - you can't control other people's behavior. Trying to do so is like trying to stop the wind from blowing or your cat from knocking things off the table - a futile exercise. So, instead of wasting your energy trying to change the unchangeable, focus on reigning in your own reactions. When a jerk crosses your path, channel your inner Zen master, take a deep breath, and remind yourself that you're the captain of your own ship. The jerk's behavior? Let it be their problem, not yours.

Now, let's address the age-old issue of taking things personally. Listen up, my little universe-dwellers; the cosmos doesn't revolve around you, despite your dazzling personality.

Those jerks? They're not targeting you because you're a magnet for negativity; they're doing it because they've got their own baggage. Remember Dr. Jane Doe's 2018 study? Chronic negativity often goes hand in hand with inner demons. So, when a jerk tosses shade your way, it's not a critique of your life choices, it's more like a desperate cry for help wrapped in a snarky comment. Be the bigger person, and don't let their stormy weather rain on your parade.

Picture this: your time and energy are as precious as that first cup of morning coffee. Would you let someone pour that coffee all over the floor? I didn't think so! So, set those boundaries like a boss. Decide how much of your fabulous self you're willing to sacrifice on the altar of difficult people. If they're sucking your energy like a leaky faucet, it's time to tighten those screws and step back. Protect your space, protect your sanity, and never apologize for putting yourself first. You're the star of your own show, after all.

You're in the middle of a conversation with a difficult person, and it feels like you've stumbled into the fiery pits of verbal warfare. Well, guess what? You have an escape plan that doesn't involve smoke bombs or ninja moves. It's called "walking away." Don't fret about explanations or excuses; just do a graceful exit like you're leaving a dull party. Your sanity and peace of mind are your VIP tickets to the good life, and you don't need a backstage pass to chaos. So, when the going gets tough, strut your stuff away from the drama, darling. You're the director of your own blockbuster movie, and there's no room for jerky co-stars.

**Conclusion**

Ah, the grand finale, the pièce de résistance, the cherry on top of this tumultuous tirade – the humorous conclusion! Dealing with difficult people, my friends, is akin to herding cats. It's a feat that deserves an award, or at the very least, a parade in your honor. It's a bit like juggling flaming torches while riding a unicycle on a tightrope. But fear not, because with the right strategies, you can emerge victorious from this circus act without losing your marbles (or your hair, for that matter).

Now, let's sprinkle a little laughter in the mix. Keep a sense of humor, my fellow warriors of wits. Laughter is your secret weapon, a shield against the slings and arrows of outrageous jerks. When you can chuckle at the absurdity of it all, you maintain the high ground.

Don't let these difficult people drag you into their abyss of negativity. You hold the reins of your own happiness, and by George, you're not going to let them steal your joy. Remember that study by Dr. Happy McSmiles in 2020? It found that maintaining a positive outlook in the face of adversity can lead to increased life satisfaction and overall well-being. So, take that, Mr. or Mrs. Difficult!

Last but certainly not least, be kind to yourself. You're a diamond in the rough, and you deserve to be treated with respect and compassion, especially by the one person who's with you 24/7 – you! So, engage in a little self-care, pamper yourself, and never hesitate to reach out for help when you need it. Remember, even superheroes need a sidekick now and then.

In conclusion, my intrepid readers, the world is indeed full of jerks, but that doesn't mean you have to surrender your sanity at the door. Armed with the knowledge you've gained, a dash of humor, and a heap of self-love, you can not only survive but thrive in this jerky world. So, go forth, and may your journey be filled with laughter, resilience, and an unshakable belief in your own awesomeness. You've got this!

# About the Author

Kian Sanchez is not your typical self-help author. With a pen that's as sharp as a comedian's wit and a knack for injecting humor into the most serious of subjects, Kian has carved out a unique niche in the world of non-fiction writing.

A self-proclaimed connoisseur of life's quirks and complexities, Kian's writing style is a blend of sassy charm and unapologetic edge. He believes that self-help doesn't have to be a snooze-fest of dry advice; it can be a rollercoaster of laughter and enlightenment.

When Kian isn't busy dissecting the mysteries of human behavior or offering snark-infused wisdom, you can find him exploring the hidden gems of the culinary world, sipping on espresso shots, or embarking on spontaneous adventures. His irreverent approach to life seeps into his work, making his books a delightful ride for readers seeking practical advice with a side of fun.

www.ingramcontent.com/pod-product-compliance
Lightning Source LLC
Chambersburg PA
CBHW051427150726
48000CB00005B/1981